DEC 0 9 2004

745
P288d
c.1

WITHDRAWN

Do not remove "date due" card
(25¢ fine if lost)

THE HACKLEY PUBLIC LIBRARY
MUSKEGON, MICHIGAN

PLEASE RETURN THIS BOOK PROMPTLY

Do not lend it to others.
Each borrower is held responsible for ALL books charged on his card.
Your co-operation and thoughtfulness help the Library give better service to all.

DEMCO

DECORATING WITH PLANT CRAFTS AND NATURAL MATERIALS

DECORATING WITH PLANT CRAFTS AND NATURAL MATERIALS

Phyllis Pautz

Doubleday & Company, Inc.
Garden City, New York   1971

To my family

Library of Congress Catalog Card Number 70-150912
Copyright © 1971 by Phyllis Pautz
All Rights Reserved
Printed in the United States of America
First Edition

Contents

Please note that an index of the specific nature crafts and projects described in this book will be found in the back, following an index to all illustrations—drawings by the author, photographs, and color plates following page 128.

Introduction   8

Chapter One   **The Natural Crafts**   13
Garden flowers, vines, shrubs, and trees to cultivate for natural decorating. Other sources of natural materials. Getting acquainted with the natural world. Seasonal calendar for natural crafts. Mail order sources.

Chapter Two   **Fresh Flowers**   *31*
Origins of favorite flowers. Folklore. Some floral messages: the language of flowers. Garden flowers for decorating. Selecting florist flowers. Best buys by season. Cutting, conditioning, making cut flowers last longer. Natural flower arranging. Borrowing naturalness from the Japanese. Technique and selection of flowers for miniatures. Decorating suggestions. Mail order sources.

Chapter Three **Dried Flowers and Pods** *53*
Historical background. Methods for drying: borax and corn meal, sand, silica gel, hanging, pressing, natural drying. When and where to collect flowers for drying. How to make a framed flower "print." Techniques for miniatures, for period bouquets. Decorating suggestions. Mail order sources.

Chapter Four **Foliage** *81*
Folklore. Historical background. Collecting, cutting, conditioning. Prolonging the cut life of all foliage. Selecting florist foliage. Forcing spring branches. Preserving foliage with glycerine. Drying autumn leaves. Techniques for drying grasses, vines, strap leaves, and branches. Decorating ideas. Mail order sources.

Chapter Five **Houseplants** *103*
General cultural needs. Simple propagating. Origins. Easy plants for home decorating. Indoor herb garden. Plants for fragrance. Forcing spring flowering bulbs. Do-it-yourself plants from kitchen leftovers. Miniatures. Terrariums. Hanging baskets. Mail order sources.

Chapter Six **Fruits and Vegetables** *127*
Origins. Folklore. Decorative uses of the past. Sources. Selection. Overlooked possibilities. Conditioning. Treating. Drying. Decorative stringing of dried vegetables. Fruits and vegetables for miniatures. Ideas for centerpieces. Decorating suggestions. Keeping abilities of fruits and vegetables for arrangements.

Chapter Seven **Driftwood** *145*
Background. Sources: countryside, florist, home garden, seashore. Collecting. Conditioning. Treating. Bleaching. Shapes and sizes with decorating possibilities. Hanging driftwood and other decorative ideas. Miniatures. Mail order sources.

Chapter Eight **Pine Cones** *161*
Year-round decorating ideas for pine cones. Collecting and other sources. Drying. Treating. Cutting pine cone flowers. Wiring. Decorating suggestions. How to make a Christmas wreath. How to make a plaque. Mail order sources.

Chapter Nine   **Fragrance**   *177*
Natural fragrance in your home. Customs of the past. Folklore. How to dry: flower petals, citrus peel, fragrant leaves. How to make an herb bowl. Recipes and instructions for potpourri and sachet. Pomander balls. Suggestions for fragrance in home decorating. Mail order sources.

Chapter Ten   **Decorating with Natural Materials**   *193*
Your home: the sum of all its parts. Natural materials inside and out. Color. Texture. Fragrant accents. Seasonal emphasis. Appropriate containers. A portfolio of interiors. Mail order sources.

A Personal Reading List   *229*

Index of Illustrations   *232*

Index of Nature Craft Projects   *238*

Introduction

I remember my grandmother's garden where tall Cosmos grew along the white picket fence. Clumps of Hollyhocks stood beside the back door and Morning Glories climbed and then covered the back porch. In the back garden, Pansies and Strawflowers and Thrift grew near the Lilac bushes. There were herbs and other plants I've forgotten, but I haven't forgotten my grandmother's feeling for each plant in her garden. She enjoyed wandering among them at dusk and in the very early morning while her breakfast tea steeped. On mornings I like to remember, I would join her and we would walk together, stopping at this plant and that to see how it was getting along. She would bend stiffly over a bud to see if it was any closer to becoming a flower than it had been the day before. Sometimes she would pick a piece of Rosemary and sniff its fragrance as she crushed it in her hand. She carried a pair of scissors on a long ribbon that was attached to her clothing in some way, and as we walked, she would snip a sample flower or two or some sprigs of Mint or a stem of foliage from the Lilacs. As the day became more clearly defined, the collection of garden samples grew. Inevitably when we returned to the house, our shoes were soaked with dew and the tea had steeped too long, but every morning we had a fresh bouquet of flowers.

My grandmother never consciously arranged flowers. She would hold them in her hand a few minutes as if to see what she had. Then she would clip some of the extra long stems, turn the bouquet around, shift a flower or two, and place them in one of her glass vases. There was no more than that to any of the bouquets that added so much color and charm to her home. The simple arrangements expressed my grandmother's love for her garden and her pleasure in the shape and color of each flower and leaf. Decorating with natural materials is just a way of enjoying part of the natural world in one's home in a satisfying and appropriate manner. If your home is a modern apartment, your choice of natural materials may be different than my grandmother's, but the motivating factors behind your choice could be the same.

From the time that man discovered he could stay in one place and grow food instead of moving about to hunt it, his life has been bound closely to the plant world. Tall rugged trees were his first deities. The leaves and roots and fruits of plants provided food for life and medicine for the ailments that afflicted him. We don't know when the first flower or branch of leaves or perfect piece of fruit was admired for its beauty alone, but this pleasant contemplation was very much a part of life in ancient Egypt, two thousand years before the birth of Christ. Baskets of fruits and vegetables were displayed at Egyptian banquets, and flowers and leaves were made into decorative wreaths and garlands. The people of ancient Rome strewed fragrant flower petals and leaves on the floors of their homes and placed pots of fragrant flowers in their courtyards. Baskets of flowers with their foliage were displayed decoratively. Greek mythology included floral legends which were to influence the flower symbolism of the Elizabethans and the flower language of the Victorians.

Contemporary decorating with natural materials includes these classical influences as well as those of Japan and China, where decorating with flowers and foliage and other plant materials has had more than a thousand-year history. The homely customs of our colonial forebears and the more formal decorating customs of the old world they left behind are part of our heritage too. To decorate our homes in today's world we should have some interest in what has gone before as well as confidence in our own taste and preferences. Most important, we must allow our feeling for natural materials to determine their selection and display.

Today there is a new and growing interest in the form and texture of natural materials. Dried pods and grasses, simply arranged, add distinctive decorative effects to modern as well as period interiors. The old-fashioned plant crafts are enjoying a revival as more people discover the satisfaction of working with natural materials and enjoy the results. This book is an attempt to make decorating with natural materials as pleasant and easy as it should be. There are detailed directions for all the natural crafts and ideas for using natural materials decoratively in each chapter as well as a portfolio of photographs in the final chapter, devoted to decorating with natural materials. If you garden, many natural materials can be grown and crafted at home. If you don't garden, visits to rural areas, the florist, and the produce market supplemented by the mail order sources listed at the end of each chapter can bring all the materials discussed in the book to you.

DECORATING WITH PLANT CRAFTS AND NATURAL MATERIALS

Chapter One

The Natural Crafts

The natural crafts—growing, collecting, processing, and arranging natural materials—can be a year-round hobby. The seasonal calendar at the end of this chapter suggests the best seasons for enjoying many of the craft activities and indicates the chapter where directions and discussion for each can be found.

Any craft must begin with the proper supplies—where to find them, how to use them. If you garden, you can, if you wish, grow many of your own materials. The following list is a sampling of plants and shrubs and some trees that will provide a good variety, enough when processed to keep any home decorated in season throughout the year. It is a limited list, though, intended only as an indication of what anyone with a little garden space might grow. Different areas will have different plant materials, and different people, different selections. Take a minute to record your own favorites, using the craft headings. Consider the limitations and special treats of your local area, then, before attempting to cultivate new plants, check a regional gardening guide for their growing requirements.

A Sampling of Plants to Cultivate for Decorating

For cut Flowers
    Chrysanthemums in variety
    Marigolds in variety
    Roses: Sweetheart
      Charlotte Armstrong
    Statice

Foliage for Fresh Arrangements
    Rhododendron
    Ivy
    Needled Evergreens
    Ferns

Branches for Forcing
    Dogwood
    Forsythia
    Pussy Willow

Decorative Wood
    Coral Dogwood (*Cornus alba*)
    Hazelnut
      (*Corylus Avellana contorta*)

Berries
    Bayberry (*Myrica pennsylvanica*)
    Bittersweet (*Celastrus scandens*)

Fragrance
    Scented-leaved Geraniums
    Rosemary
    Damask Rose (*Rosa damascena*)
    Lavender

Flowers for Drying
    Statice
    Strawflowers in variety
    Yarrow
    Pansies
    Violets

Foliage for Drying and Pressing
    Pussy Willow
    Ornamental grasses
    Wheat
    Ferns

Foliage for Fall Color, Dried or Fresh
    Dogwood
    Beech

Vegetables for Drying
    Gourds in variety
    Ornamental Corn

Pods
    Chinese Lanterns (*Physalis Alkekengi*)
    Honesty (*Lunaria*)

Pine trees for cones

I've listed Chrysanthemums and Marigolds under cut flowers, because they are easy to grow, freely blooming, and, most important, the cut flowers are long lasting when conditioned as described in Chapter Two. Perennial Chrysanthemums are available in a wide selection of kinds, colors, and sizes. Taking advantage of this variety will provide blooms from midsummer into the late fall when everything else has faded. Marigolds are annuals and must be reseeded or replanted each year, but they bloom fairly early and, when cut regularly, continue blooming throughout the summer. Dwarf varieties of Marigolds and Chrysanthemums are particularly attractive as border edgings. Larger sizes can be grown in the shrub or perennial border or in the cutting garden.

The two varieties of Roses were chosen for their long cut life. They will do best in the Rose garden where, in common with all Roses, their needs for absolutely full sun and rich, well-drained soil can be met. Here, too, should go the Damask Rose. This lovely old Rose has a very short blooming period, but the long-lasting fragrance of its dried petals is a valuable addition to sachet and potpourri mixtures. Lavender, listed under Fragrance, makes an attractive border for the Rose garden. Its fragrant leaves and petals, when dried, add a spicy scent to the potpourri jar. Directions for making potpourri and other fragrant delights can be found in Chapter Nine. Scented-leaved Geraniums and Rosemary from the Fragrance list are easily cultivated in pots. They can be enjoyed on the patio or sunk into the garden in summer to be returned to the house when the weather cools. Better still, if space permits, you might want to plan a small herb garden, with

Tyron Palace and gardens, Tyron, North Carolina: one lovely extreme in the range of garden styles.

pot herbs for culinary flavoring and additional fragrant herbs. Mint, Sweet Woodruff, Lemon Verbena, and Thyme are just a few that might be included with the Rosemary and scented-leaved Geraniums. A planting of Lavender would be appropriate here as well. Several excellent books devoted entirely to herbs are listed at the end of this book. These give detailed directions for planning herb gardens based on monastery plantings of the past or eighteenth-century knot gardens as well as more contemporary designs.

Pansies and Violets listed under Flowers for Drying are delightful when dried and arranged in old-fashioned framed flower "prints." Directions for making the "prints" are in Chapter Three. Violets are available in several different varieties and colors and are so easily grown that without control they may take over your garden. They are attractive planted under late-leafing shrubs, where their early spring flowers softly color the bare garden landscape. Pansies are another Viola. Although they are perennials, too, they do best if they are replanted each year. Pansies like moist, well-drained soil and cool weather. They make attractive border edgings, and if the flowers are cut regularly, their blooming period can be somewhat prolonged.

Bayberry, Pussy Willow, and Bittersweet, along with Ivy and the other shrubs listed under Foliage for Fresh Arrangements, can be enjoyed for their landscaping effect in the garden and pruned judiciously to provide decorative material for the house. The Christmas Fern, sometimes called Wood Fern, is easy to grow in dry or slightly moist, shady places under trees or tall shrubs. These are delightful when arranged with fresh flowers or when dried and pressed, are indispensable for winter bouquets.

I like a generous planting of Strawflowers in variety. Most of these flowers must be cut for drying just before full bloom, so that their garden effect is limited. Most are annuals and must be renewed each year. They are best grown in the cutting garden. Into the cutting garden, too, should go the leggy clumps of ornamental grasses, a row or two of Wheat, and the perennial Yarrow. Off to itself a bit so that its vigorous growth can be somewhat controlled goes the Chinese Lantern plant. Honesty is a biennial that can be grown in sun or shade. Its flowers are not showy and I prefer to plant it in rows in the cutting garden.

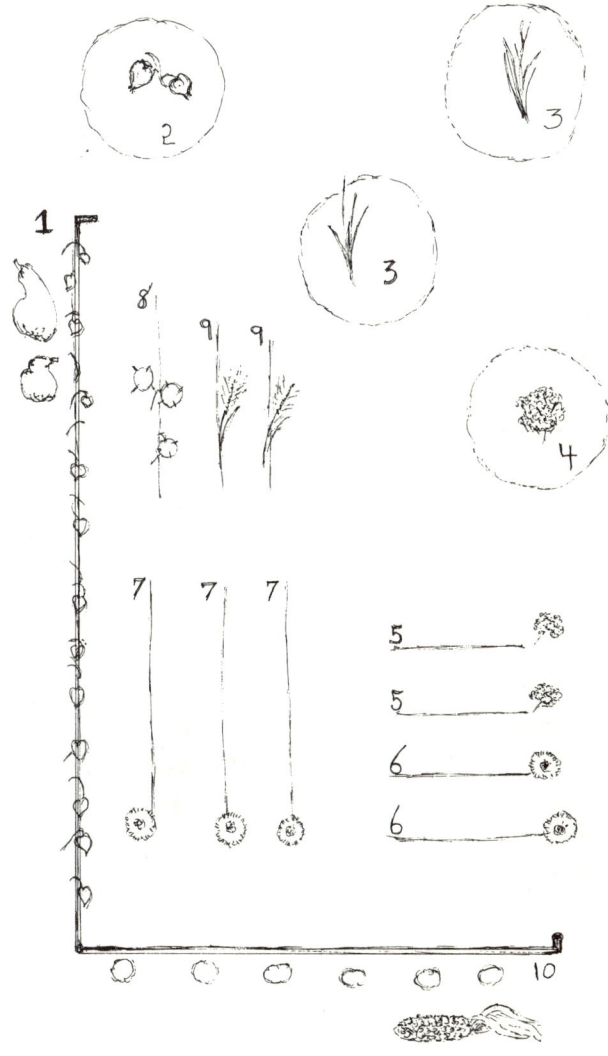

Diagram of cutting garden: 1) Gourds; 2) Chinese Lanterns; 3) ornamental grasses; 4) Yarrow; 5) Statice; 6) and 7) Strawflowers; 8) Honesty; 9) Wheat; 10) Corn.

You'll have to wait until the second year for results, after the first sowing. Then, although it will self sow, it is best to add new seeds each year to be sure of a continuing crop. These silvery pods are delightful in winter arrangements. Statice, which can be

THE NATURAL CRAFTS 17

planted in the perennial border, is as lovely in bouquets of fresh flowers as it is in dried arrangements. It seems most convenient to include it in the cutting garden where it can be gathered as needed without destroying the garden design. Directions for drying these plants and flowers are included in Chapter Three. All of the plants are easy to grow with the exception of Statice, which is sometimes difficult to get started. Excepting Honesty, all need sun and a good, well-fertilized soil. For best results, consult a regional gardening guide for cultural details.

The cutting garden can be enclosed on two sides with a sturdy trellis or low fence. Along one side can go the seeds of large and small Gourds, which will climb and cover the fence and produce their colorful crop in the fall. Along the other side a row of ornamental Corn can be planted. Both are annuals that grow fairly quickly, and the rows of seedlings should be thinned to provide growing space for the mature plants. Directions for drying and processing these two vegetables are in Chapter Six.

Almost any broad-leaved shrub can provide foliage for glycerinizing and press drying, and most, along with needled Evergreens, can provide foliage for fresh arrangements. I've included my favorites, but do experiment with what is already available in your own garden. The same is true of branches for forcing. I've listed branches that force easily, but you'll surely have your own favorites. Most branches can be forced, some more easily than others. Chapter Four lists more branches for forcing as well as those suitable for glycerinizing and pressing and directions for carrying out these procedures.

Hopefully, you have a few Pine trees of cone-bearing age in your garden, or nearby, as well as other trees with foliage that colors in the fall. If you are adding new trees to your garden, a regional garden guide will be indispensable to help you choose those that will thrive in your local environment. I've included the lovely, versatile Dogwood tree on my list. It has a wide growing range and is a source of decorative material all through the year: bare branches for forcing in late winter, flowering branches in spring, green leaves for foliage arrangements in summer, and softly tinted autumn leaves to be enjoyed fresh or pressed and dried for permanent arrangements. For a bonus, the

Dogwood produces red berries in fall to attract songbirds to your garden.

Many different trees and shrubs will provide decorative wood, but the Hazelnut (*Corylus Avellana contorta*) is really a conversation piece. Its intricately twisted branches are amazing to see, and when cut and arranged in a floor standing container they make an intriguing display.

If garden space is limited, you can select specimen plants and still have a fairly extensive supply of natural materials. A few can be grown in containers as houseplants. A tiny plot, well planned, can yield an adequate amount for decorative purposes. It takes only a few grains of Wheat, for instance, to provide enough stalks for a winter bouquet.

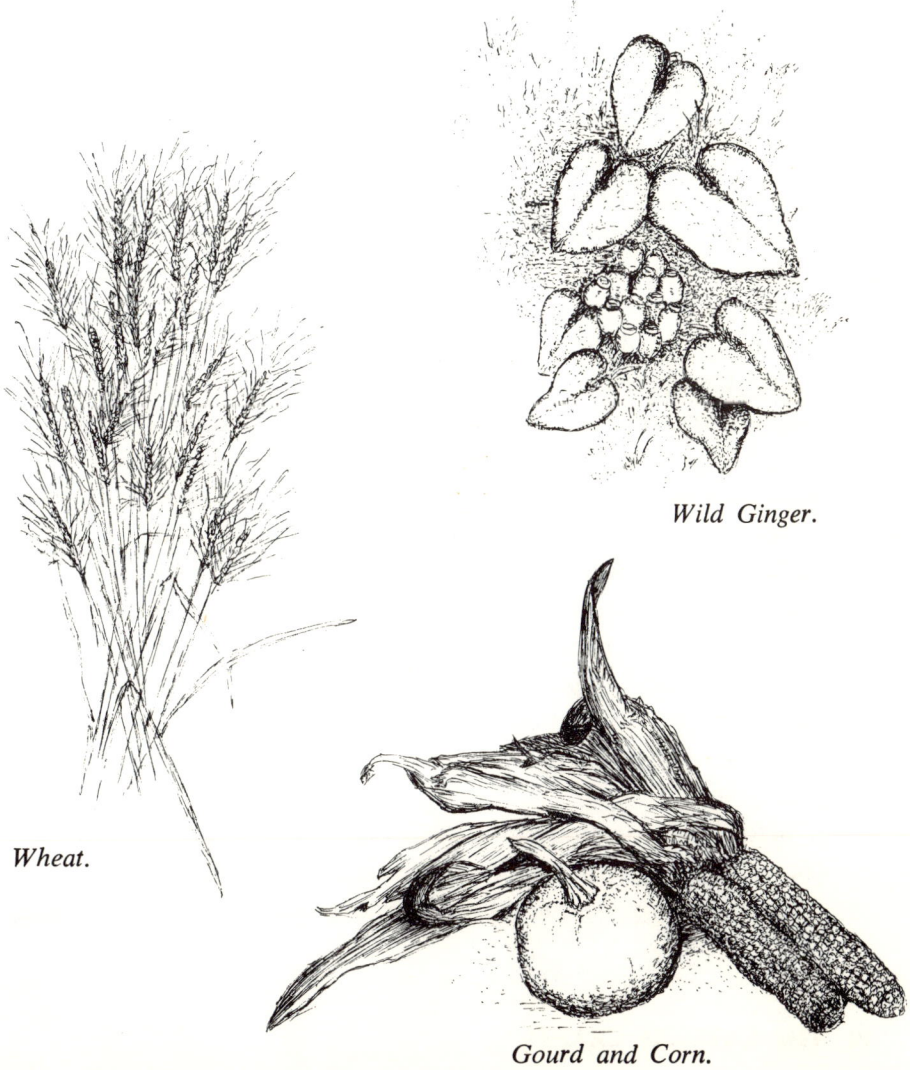

Wild Ginger.

Wheat.

Gourd and Corn.

If you don't have a garden, mail order sources and a good florist can supply many natural materials for your home. Even when you do garden, the florist can bring you plant materials that are difficult or impossible to cultivate in your own area. He can usually supply driftwood, fresh and processed foliage, dried flowers, and of course lovely cut flowers the year round. Look around until you find a flower shop that is pleasant just to be in. Then visit it regularly. Take time to browse and ask questions. Learn the names of unfamiliar flowers and foliages. If you include a small purchase with your visit, perhaps Eucalyptus for glycerinizing or a small bunch of lemon leaf, your education will probably progress most graciously. In addition to the florist, gift shops and the decorating accessory departments of large stores frequently offer unusual dried pods and grasses, branches of processed Eucalyptus and dried Wheat, grasses and Strawflowers and Starflowers.

A vegetable market can provide most of the fruits and vegetables you need for immediate decorating and for drying, as well as dried Corn and Gourds in season. Choose this source of supply as carefully as you do the florist. Look for a variety of fresh produce, attractively displayed, in a clean, good-smelling store. With its medley of colors and fragrances, the market should be as pleasant to visit as the florist.

For the gardener and non-gardener alike, the best hunting grounds for natural materials are in the countryside; but you do have to learn to see the treasures that are waiting. If you don't have a close acquaintance with the natural world you may want to read one or two of the books listed under The Natural World on the reading list at the end of this book. Any one of them can give you a new awareness of the natural landscape. Visit state and federal parks to become aware of the infinite variety of plant materials. Observe the different textures and contours of plants and flowers and trees and shrubs. You can't pick anything, of course, but gradually you will find yourself acquiring an educated eye.

Before collecting natural materials anywhere, you should consult conservation lists to determine the plants that are protected and must be left to grow and multiply. These lists are usually available

Vermont Road.

from state, park, or conservation, departments as well as local garden clubs. They contain the names of plants that are disappearing because they have been ruthlessly overpicked or have not been able to hold their own in the face of encroaching civilization. Many of the protected plants are available now from mail order nurseries listed at the end of this chapter. You can if you wish order them for your own garden, thus providing your home with a sampling of unusual decorative materials as well as aiding in the conservation of threatened plants.

Well informed and well prepared, you will enjoy a collecting expedition immeasurably more. Take a train or bus or drive, but do try to visit a rural area at least seasonally. Take along an old pair of shoes for tramping, a pair of clippers, and a basket stuffed with wet paper toweling in a plastic bag to keep plant materials fresh. Carry a guide to local wild flowers with good clear photographs of the individual flowers, and enjoy getting acquainted with the lovely plants you see. To the even slightly educated eye, the tangle of weeds along the roadside becomes a collection of wild plants of many forms, textures, and gradations of color. In winter, interesting pieces of driftwood are exposed. A closer inspection reveals pods and branches in colors that vary from mahogany brown to soft rust to pale beige and gray. In spring, the earliest wild flowers appear, close to the ground among the fallen leaves and dried stalks of the previous year. Small Ferns put touches of green on the still bare ground, and you may discover the wild Ginger which later will produce tiny brown jugs beneath its leaves. In early summer, gather armfuls of Queen Anne's Lace and later, discover Goldenrod and Joe-Pye Weed and the other escapees from early American gardens that color the roadside and dry beautifully.

The best areas for collecting natural materials are the rights of way along rural roads. But pick sparingly and always leave some flowers to reseed themselves. Don't drag anything out by its roots. Most owners of undeveloped woodlands and meadows and even empty suburban lots will be gracious about allowing you to gather the more prolific wild flowers like Goldenrod and Queen Anne's Lace, if you ask first.

Become aware of those areas that are marked for desecration by the bulldozer for housing developments and new roads. Your local newspaper will usually have advance information about projects of this kind. Where progress and money are involved, the conservation lists are ignored, yet these condemned areas are often storehouses of rare plants as well as other natural materials. If you garden, you should lift protected plants before they are destroyed, and bring them to the safety of your own garden for conservation purposes as well as your own pleasure.

An interest in natural materials can turn your vacation trip into a treasure hunt. Write ahead to departments of tourism in the states or countries you plan to visit and ask for information about their state parks and wilderness areas and public gardens. Then explore these areas away from home to gain firsthand knowledge of unfamiliar plants and trees and shrubs. Visit local shops when you travel, to find unusual dried plant materials, local pine cones and driftwood, natural feathers and rocks and stones and, if you are near the coast, sea shells. These materials can be used in arrangements or as appropriate accessories with other natural materials.

Visit the shops and studios of local craftsmen everywhere to find unusual containers. A craft directory that can be ordered by mail is listed at the end of this chapter. Do send for it. There are craft shops and studios in almost every state. Some are just

Stone Soldier Pottery; Jacksonville, Vermont.

THE NATURAL CRAFTS 23

The Loom Room, Durham, North Carolina.

a few miles off the thruway, but without advance knowledge, you won't know they exist. Today's crafts have developed from the handcrafted articles our ancestors made for utilitarian purposes. In many sections of the country, crafts were revived because people were concerned that the old procedures were being forgotten. The craft revival provided residents of many depressed areas with a means of supporting themselves. Today many of the original craftsmen have been joined by more sophisticated artists who enjoy doing the work they love at their own pace. The beautifully executed wood work and ceramics are especially compatible with natural plant materials.

To its thousands of practitioners, one of the most fascinating natural crafts is flower arrangement: placing flowers in creatively designed arrangements for exhibition and prizes as well as home decoration. Garden clubs have led the way in the development of this craft, setting high standards of design and requiring plant materials of excellent quality and condition. At her best, the floral arranger considers the growth habits and natural appearance of the flowers and other plant materials to be displayed and then creates an appropriate design for their display. When this is not the case, the natural loveliness of the flowers suffers. The crescent shape, so popular a few years ago, was frequently used not as a guide but as an end in itself. Flowers were often distorted in an effort to carry out the line. The S curve, Hogarth's "line of beauty" was another popular design and must still be considered an excellent skeleton on which to build an arrangement. Used as design guides and no more, both can result in beautifully creative arrangements. A deep interest in this craft can best be served by joining a garden club, taking lessons from a competent floral designer, and practicing with a good basic flower arranging book before going on to create original designs of your own. Blue ribbons are still being awarded in the best shows for the most creative arrangements executed with a clear understanding of design principles as well as an understanding of the plant materials. To excel requires serious study.

In this book, emphasis is placed on a relaxed approach toward natural materials and on a simple unarranged effect for their display in the home. If you have picked up this book, you probably have an inherent feeling for natural materials. A little practice with confidence in your own taste should find you producing arrangements and groupings of plant materials that are right for your home. Suggestions for natural flower arranging are given in Chapter Two. In addition, you may want to read more about the entire subject. Four books are suggested on the reading list at the end of the book.

Enjoying the natural crafts is a pleasant pastime, but a new and intimate awareness of the natural world may be an unexpected bonus.

Seasonal Calendar
For Collecting and Processing Natural Materials

Spring
    Forcing flowering
        branches   Chapter Four
    Drying early spring
        flowers   Chapter Three
    Collecting driftwood   Chapter Seven
    Pressing green leaves and
        ferns   Chapter Four
    Glycerinizing florist and
        fresh foliage   Chapter Four
    Collecting and drying
        wild flowers   Chapter Three
Summer
    Drying flowers   Chapter Three
    Drying fragrant petals and
        leaves for potpourri   Chapter Nine
    Collecting and propagat-
        ing plant slips   Chapter Five
    Glycerinizing some foliages Chapter Four
    Collecting pine cones   Chapter Eight
    Drying fragrant herbs   Chapter Nine
    Collecting pods for drying   Chapter Three
    Drying some fruits and
        vegetables   Chapter Six

Fall
    Drying gourds — Chapter Six
    Collecting pine cones — Chapter Eight
    Collecting driftwood — Chapter Seven
    Collecting naturally dried wild plants — Chapter Three
    Drying autumn leaves — Chapter Four
    Drying ornamental vegetables — Chapter Six
    Drying fruits and vegetables from the market — Chapter Six
    Glycerinizing foliage from the florist — Chapter Four

Winter
    Forcing spring flowering bulbs — Chapter Five
    Collecting bare branches — Chapter Seven
    Collecting driftwood — Chapter Seven
    Glycerinizing florist foliage — Chapter Four
    Drying unusual florist flowers — Chapter Three

Mail Order Sources:

Spring Hill Nurseries
Tipp City, Ohio 45371

Plants and flowers, some wild plants. Catalogue.

Geo. W. Park Seed Co., Inc.
Greenwood, S.C. 29646

Plants and seeds. Good selection of strawflowers. Some wild flowers. Grasses, gourds. Catalogue.

The Wayside Gardens
Mentor, Ohio 44060

Some everlastings. Some wild flowers. Trees and shrubs. Spring flowering bulbs. Catalogue—not free but refundable with order.

Special Sources:

Merry Gardens
Camden, Maine 04843

Herb plants, scented-leaved geraniums.

Putney Nursery, Inc.
Putney, Vt. 05346

Wild flowers. Ferns. Herbs.

Cook's Geranium Nursery
Lyons, Kans. 67554

Scented-leaved geraniums.

Tillotson's Roses
Brown's Valley Road
Watsonville, Calif. 95076

Old-fashioned fragrant roses.

Craft Shops, U.S.A.

A directory of craftsmen in the continental United States, Alaska, and Hawaii.

The American Crafts Council   *There is a charge for the directory.*
29 W. 53rd St.
New York, N.Y. 10019

Chapter Two

Fresh Flowers

Flowers are world travelers. Most of our old favorites originated in Asia and gradually made their way through Asia Minor to Europe, centuries before the birth of Christ. They traveled with nomadic tribes and traders, sometimes carried purposely but often as seeds clinging to clothing and packed in belongings. Our garden Rose is a descendant of a cultivated Rose that was familiar to the ancient Egyptians. The Carnation, Narcissus, Iris, Violet, and many of the Lilies have shared our turbulent history for well over a thousand years. Hollyhocks, familiar flowers in colonial dooryards, are natives of China. They were enjoyed in English gardens for at least a century before the colonists brought them to the new world. Bouncing Bet and wild Yarrow grow as profusely along our roadsides as any native wild flower, but they were brought here in colonial times for practical reasons. The Yarrow was the principal ingredient in several tonics. Bouncing Bet was a substitute for soap. If you crush the stems and leaves in water you can work up a slight lather of rather dubious cleansing abilities. The Geranium and the Gladiola are natives of South

Heartsease.

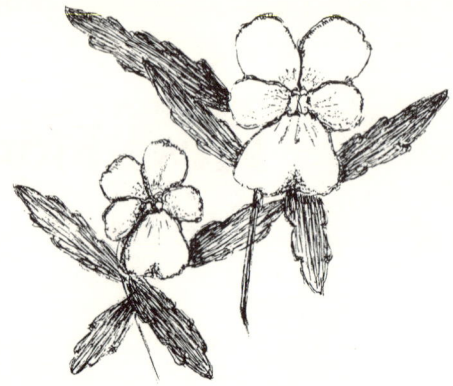

Africa and came here with the early settlers. Our charming Pansy is a hybrid result of crossbreeding between members of the Violet family. Shakespeare's Heartsease is one of its ancestors. The Petunia was discovered growing wild in Brazil early in the nineteenth century. The Dahlia began its world tour in Mexico.

Some flowers followed indirect routes to their destinations. The African and French Marigolds, variations of the same native Mexican plant, were sent unnamed to Spain shortly after the exploration of Mexico. The African Marigold turned up next in North Africa. From there it was carried to England where it was assumed that it was a native of North Africa and named accordingly. The French Marigold was sent from Spain to France. Probably the Huguenots brought it to England. To further confuse matters, the Calendula, a flower of somewhat similar appearance, had used the name Pot Marigold for a century before the colorful Mexicans arrived. All three Marigolds traveled to North America with the English colonists where the flowers of the Pot Marigold continued to be used to flavor soups and stews as they had in the old world.

The road of plant travel ran both ways. Coreopsis and Phlox were growing wild in the new world when the colonists arrived. Their seeds and roots were sent to England where they became established garden flowers. Surprisingly, Goldenrod was another native American that became a garden success in England. Cultivating the rampant weed was almost a fad among fashionable

English gardeners in the eighteenth century. Its popularity has passed but an improved variety is still grown in English gardens.

Since antiquity, flowers have been the source of legends and fancies. The Greeks ascribed symbolic messages to many flowers. Centuries later the Elizabethans revived some of these classical sentiments. Shakespeare's, "There's Rosemary, that's for remembrance," is one example of a widespread interest. It remained for the Victorians to make flowers talk. The language of flowers seems to have come to Europe from the Persian court in the eighteenth century, an elegant amusement that the Victorians elevated to absurdity. Sentimental phrases were assigned to individual flowers. It became possible to send all kinds of coy messages without writing a word. Tiny floral dictionaries enjoyed a lively commerce. Ladies and gentlemen on both sides of the Atlantic published books outlining the most subtle nuances of floral translation. Combinations of flowers were given specific meanings. The color of a flower altered its message. A bud symbolized something different than the full bloom of the same flower. There were petulant debates between the hard book covers over the authenticity of rival definitions. Finally the whole gentle nonsense succumbed in a muddle of meanings, late in the nineteenth century.

The Victorians delighted in arranging tuzzie-muzzies according to the language of flowers. These tiny nosegays had been enjoyed by the Elizabethans for their fragrance, but the Victorian bouquet conveyed true sentiment. A central flower would be chosen for the main thought. Perhaps a red Rose for love. The Rose would then be surrounded with smaller flowers to amplify the main sentiment. The small bouquet was usually placed in a lace-paper holder and presented to a friend who hopefully consulted a copy of the floral dictionary you had used. If you are in a whimsical mood some day, you may want to make a tuzzie-muzzie of your own. Arrangements based on the tuzzie-muzzie can be made in any size. A large one would be an attractive centerpiece for a bridal shower or luncheon. Tiny matching tuzzie-muzzie bouquets could be placed at each setting as favors for the guests. To make the centerpiece size, you'll need a low round white bowl. Place it upside down on a round white lace-paper doily and with a pencil trace around the bowl. Remove

FRESH FLOWERS 33

the bowl and cut the traced circle from the center of the doily. Now stuff the bowl with water-soaked Oasis and slip the doily over the bowl. Tape the edges of the doily to the rim of the bowl. Use one or more Roses depending on the size of your arrangement. Cut their stems short, remove the foliage, and place them upright in the center of the container. Choose additional flowers from the sample dictionary of meanings that follows, and place these flowers with stems cut short around the Roses. If your container is large you may want to use several different flowers, but distribute them evenly around the arrangement. Complete the arrangement with sprigs of Rose or other small-leaved foliage tucked in among the smaller flowers.

Use small lace-paper doilies for the matching bouquets. You'll need just one Rose and a sampling of the smaller flowers used in the centerpiece. Cut a hole in the doily and slip it over the stems up under the flower heads. Tape in place. Place the short stems in an orchid tube or water pick filled with water. A pretty satin bow will complete these tuzzie-muzzie bouquets. Lay them at each place setting, arranging the doily so that it covers the water pick.

Tuzzie-muzzie: centerpiece and matching bouquet.

The Language of Flowers

Anemone	*Go away*
Aster	*Elegance*
Azalea	*Delicate passions*
Camellia	*My love is forever*
Canterbury Bell	*Beware*
Daisy	*I am innocent*
Forget-Me-Not	*My faithful love*
Gardenia	*My secret love*
Geranium	*You are foolish*
Goldenrod	*Good fortune will come to you*
Heliotrope	*My devoted friend*
Hollyhock	*You are ambitious*
Iris	*I have hope*
Jonquil	*My passionate desire*
Lavender	*My undying love*
Marigold	*What is wrong?*
Mignonette	*Your modest beauty*
Morning Glory	*Farewell*
Narcissus	*You are too proud*
Pansy	*Pensive thoughts*
Petunia	*I am angry*
Poppy	*Daydream*
Rose, Red	*I love you*
Rose, White	*You are so pure*
Strawflower	*Everlasting*
Sweet William	*My gallant friend*
Tuberose	*Forbidden pleasures*
Violet	*Modesty becomes you*

Long-lasting Cut Flowers

All flowers are lovely, but unless we choose those that with reasonable care can adjust to living for a while in water, their beauty will be short lived. Too many bouquets collapsing after a short life can take the fun from decorating with fresh flowers. The list that follows is a guide to selecting flowers for long-lasting

decorative uses. Only wild and cultivated flowers that will last a week or more after cutting are included. Those that are starred should last two weeks or longer. Most of the lovely spring flowering bulbs aren't mentioned, and some of your favorites may not be found. Most cut flowers will last at least three or four days. You can enjoy these in small accent bouquets which are more easily changed. Arrange them, too, with long-lasting foliage and remove just the flowers as they fade.

Flowers That Will Last a Week or More after Cutting

Especially long lasting
- Anemone
- *Anthurium
- Aster
- Bells-of-Ireland
- Black-Eyed Susan
- Calla Lily
- Canterbury Bells
- *Carnation
- *Chrysanthemum
- Coreopsis
- Daffodil
- *Daisy
- English Daisy
- Feverfew
- Heliotrope
- Gladiolus
- Globe Amaranth
- *Goldenrod
- *Heather
- Larkspur
- Lavender
- Lemon Verbena
- Lilac
- *Marigold
- Meadow Rue
- Nigella
- Peony
- Phlox
- Queen Anne's Lace
- Ranunculus
- Roses:
  - Charlotte Armstrong
  - Crimson Glory
  - Peace
  - Radiance
  - Sweetheart
- Salvia
- Snapdragon
- *Statice
- Sweet William
- Torch Lily
- Tuberose
- Yarrow
- *Zinnia
- *Most flowering herbs

*asually overflowing bouquet at home in
istinguished setting.*

FRESH FLOWERS 37

Lilac, Hyacinths, and Narcissus arranged in delft crocus pot by Miss Edna Pennell for Colonial Williamsburg.

Conditioning Cut Flowers

The life of all cut flowers is directly influenced by the time of day they are collected, how they are cut, and the treatment they receive directly after cutting. Like the list above, the following suggestions are not intended to deter you from snipping a few favorite flowers when you're in the mood. They do provide a guide for prolonging the life of cut flowers when a long-lasting effect is desired. If you can set aside a cupboard to store the few things you need, the procedure becomes an easily followed routine.

Collecting and Caring for Cut Flowers

You'll need

1 deep container for conditioning flowers overnight; a ten-quart plastic wastebasket is good.

1 pail with handle for collecting flowers; a lightweight plastic pail is convenient.

1 pair of small pruning shears or wire cutters; better for clean cutting than scissors or knife.

1 small watering pot with long spout; the plastic type is easy to use.

1 tin or carton commercial flower preservative; Floralife or Sta-Fresh are two excellent brands.

Procedure

1. Fill pail and conditioning container with water. Let them stand five or ten minutes to allow tiny air bubbles to escape.
2. Collect flowers just before dusk.
3. Cut stem ends at a slant.
4. Put immediately into the pail of water.
5. When you have collected enough flowers, take them inside and remove all or most of the foliage.
6. Hold stem ends under water in the large conditioning container and recut at a slant.
7. Without removing the stems from the water add more water so that it reaches to just below the flower heads.
8. Leave the flowers in the conditioning water overnight in a cool dark place.
9. In the morning, fill vases with water and add commercial preservative. (Follow directions on carton for correct amount.) Arrange flowers.
10. Check the water in the containers regularly, especially after the first twenty-four hours when flowers use the greatest amount.
11. Clean vases thoroughly in hot water and detergent after each use.

Special attention
- Use glass or pottery containers. If you must use metal for decorative reasons, place a glass container inside to hold water and flowers.
- Submerge garden and florist's Violets in cold water for five minutes to restore after premature wilting.
- Woody stems such as those of some Chrysanthemums should be crushed. Do this with a hammer and rinse stem ends under running water. Flower stems which exude liquid should be crushed and rinsed in the same manner.
- Petunias revive and have more body if you add a heaping tablespoon of sugar to a quart of conditioning water and leave them in the solution overnight. It should reach up to the flower head.
- Pennies and aspirin do not prolong the life of cut flowers.

If you like to collect wild flowers from the countryside, take along a plastic bag containing wet paper toweling or a good-sized piece of water-soaked Oasis to keep the flowers fresh. Poke holes in the Oasis with a pencil to hold the flower stems more easily. As mentioned in Chapter One, do consult the conservation lists for your area so that you don't pick protected wild flowers. The lists are usually available from local garden clubs and from your state department of parks or conservation.

Lilies massed in an earthenware jug.

Florist's Flowers

The knowledgeable selection of florist's flowers allows gardener and non-gardener alike to decorate with fresh flowers all through the year. Florist's flowers are priced by the stem and by the dozen as well as by arrangement. You should be able to buy as few of each kind of flower as you wish. Foliage is usually priced separately but it is quite inexpensive. Choose flowers that are in opening bud or just approaching full bloom. Fresh flowers are sprightly with firm petals and leaves. Check the sepals (the green cover of the bud

before it opens). If these are too withered, the flower has been open too long. The following list indicates the florist's flowers that are available at different times of the year. For the purpose of the chart, spring extends from January until May and summer from mid-April until September. Not all flowers are available for the entire period, and availability will vary somewhat with locality and florist. The best buys in florist's flowers are those with the longest cut life. These are starred on the list. Flowers must be absolutely fresh and they should be reconditioned at home. Start at step six of the Procedure for caring for cut flowers.

List of Available Florist's Flowers by Season

Flowers that should last at least a week

Available all year
*Anthurium   Lily-of-the-Valley
*Carnation   Sweetheart Roses
*Chrysanthemum   Violets
 Gladiola

Spring flowers, available January to May
  Acacia   Narcissus
  Anemone   *Snapdragon
*Bells-of-Ireland   Statice
  Calendula   Stephanotis
  Daffodil   *Stock
  Iris   Tulip
*Marigold

Summer flowers, available May to September
*Aster   Delphinium
 Baby's-Breath   Freesia
*Calla Lily   Gerbera
 Cosmos   *Ranunculus
*Daisies (various)

Fall flowers
*Chincherinchee
 Clivia   Torch Lily

42 FRESH FLOWERS

Flower Arranging

To acquire a feeling for natural flower arranging, try to visit an art museum and study the floral paintings. From the Italian masters to the French impressionists to the representational painters of today, artists have painted charming bouquets uninhibited by rules or styles of flower arrangement. Some bouquets peek over the tops of tall vases. Some seem to be overflowing small containers. Some are formal and others are casual. All are true natural arrangements that express the feeling of the artist for the flowers he painted. The next time you collect a bouquet of flowers from the florist or garden, take a minute to look at the individual flowers. Notice the form of the flower. The Rose seems to have hundreds of gently

Calendula.

curved petals, one unfolding from the other until finally the full flower appears. Tulips are willowy like too tall young girls. Narcissus and Daffodils come in seemingly endless variations. The nature of the flower and your feeling about it should determine how it is displayed.

Bouquet of Larkspur, Peonies, Cornflowers, and Daisies arranged by Miss Pennell for Colonial Williamsburg.

Natural Arrangements

Gladioli are often cut up and placed in arrangements that completely obscure their natural appearance. They look most handsome in a tall vase placed on the floor or on a bulky chest. Strip the

Gladioli.

Gladiolus leaves from the flowers. Cut the end of each flower and leaf stem to a slightly different length, without taking away much height. Put them all together and rearrange them in your hand. When you are pleased, lower the bouquet into a tall water-filled vase. The result is a dramatic splash of color which can be placed where such an effect is needed.

Good basic containers can make natural arranging easy. The column vase, the tall vase with base and rim slightly narrower than the middle, and the vase with a long neck and bulbous bottom are three to keep on hand in varying heights. Add a few short wide containers with enough depth to hold a bouquet, and decorating with fresh flowers will be easy and fun.

Tall natural arrangements can be either full or sparse. Full bouquets can consist of a bunch of Cosmos, for instance, filled out with leafy foliage. You can use a variety of forms arranged together: spikes like Delphiniums, airy clusters like Baby's-Breath, and well-defined flower heads like Daisies. Cut the stems to four or five different lengths. Hold the materials in your hand and casually distribute the different forms all around the bouquet. When you are satisfied, you can hold the bouquet next to the vase to check the effect. Too tall? Keep the bouquet together and cut the stems in varying shorter lengths. Too short? Use a shorter vase of the same shape. With a little experience you'll be able to judge the proportions as you cut the flower stems.

Experiment with natural arrangements. Try a narrow vase, six or seven inches high, with a grouping of flower heads just above the rim. Again, cut each flower stem to a slightly different length. An arrangement of this kind, reminiscent of a Redon flower painting, is delightful in a period bedroom. Choose the container carefully, to complement the room, and try using flowers of one color to match other small accessories.

Vases.

You can make a colorful natural bouquet for the breakfast table in minutes. Just cut the stems of flowers like Zinnias short and remove all the foliage. Using flowers of one color, perhaps red, place them in a short wide container with the heads close together in a small mountain of color. You usually don't need a holder for natural bouquets. The bulk of material in full bouquets will support itself. The long stems in tall sparse bouquets support each other. If you feel you must have something, crumple a little floral or chicken wire and place it inside the container to stabilize the stems.

We can borrow natural flower arranging ideas from the Japanese. A feeling for flowers and all natural materials is shared by the most

Tall natural bouquet.

Single Iris with its own foliage.

Tall Japanese bouquet.

privileged and poorest persons in Japan. Flowers are everywhere. The flower peddler calls regularly door to door. Usually a woman, she carries the flowers wrapped in damp newspaper and then in a straw mat on her back. If requested, she will select and arrange the

FRESH FLOWERS 47

A few flowers from the spring garden brighten this breakfast table.

flowers for you in your home. With only her feeling for natural things to guide her, she may select a branch of foliage, study it, remove some unnecessary twigs and leaves, and place it in your tall vase. From several Chrysanthemums, she may pick a full bloom and a bud. The stem of the bloom will be cut somewhat shorter than the stem of the bud. Then she'll place each carefully in the vase so that all stems balance and support each other.

Without formal knowledge of Japanese flower arrangement, we can share some of the Japanese feeling for natural materials. Simple arrangements using few materials emphasize the line and form of each branch and flower in a manner that is compatible with both period and contemporary interiors. The Japanese flower peddler's bouquet, above, would be an attractive accessory for an antique chest in an eighteenth-century entrance hall. In a contemporary home it would be dramatically effective placed on the floor beside a wide expanse of glass window wall. Incidentally, you might want to put a stone or other weight inside the container to stabilize it and add a small piece of crumpled chicken wire to catch the plant stems and hold them in place.

The same Japanese feeling for natural materials can be expressed in small accent bouquets using a single flower with a leaf or two in a low container. A needlepoint holder will be needed to support the plant material. These small arrangements are especially attractive on side tables and book shelves in the living room, color matched to other small accessories.

Miniatures

You gain a new perspective of the natural world when you discover the fun of making miniature bouquets. A stem of Baby's-Breath provides a cloud of airy white in a large bouquet. A small sprig is highlighted in a miniature. The tiny flowers are revealed as exact replicas of larger single blossoms. You can use all the leftovers of large bouquets and try them in many different arrangements, quickly and easily, with intriguing results. Containers for miniatures can be improvised from jar covers and perfume bottles and lipstick caps. You can have fun collecting well-designed miniatures of distinguished full-sized containers. Good proportion is the secret of attractive miniature bouquets. The relation of flower head to vase should be the same as in a full-sized bouquet. Cuticle scissors make cutting the small stems easy. An eye dropper can be used to add water to the arrangements. To hold a vertical miniature bouquet, stuff the vase with Oasis which has soaked in water containing a pinch of commercial flower preservative. Tiny needlepoint holders or the flower arranging material called Sta-Set can be used in low containers. The flowers and foliage of many herbs are long lasting and especially appropriate for miniature bouquets.

A miniature bouquet is delightful on a night table next to the bed where it will cheer the sluggish morning spirits. A tiny full bouquet of miniature flowers with a sprig or two of Rosemary or Mint tucked in for fragrance and foliage can make the grayest day seem bright. This is a refreshing accent for the guest room as well.

Mail Order Sources:

Flower arranging supplies

    Dorothy Biddle Service   *Catalogue available.*
    DBS Building
    Hawthorne, N.Y. 10532

    Garden Club Products   *Catalogue available.*
    Mapes' Garden Center
    Route 1, Kennebunk, Me. 04043

    Floral Art   *Catalogue available.*
    P. O. Box 394, Highland Sta.
    Springfield, Mass. 01109

Commercial products
Sta-Set
Sta-Fresh
    Plantabbs Corp.   *Brochure available.*
    Timonium, Md. 21093

...mall scatter bouquet of Pansies in a ...eacup adds a light touch to this study ...orner.

Chapter Three

Dried Flowers and Pods

If fresh flowers at any season remind us of springtime and the lush abundance of summer, dried flowers recall the gentle fading of fall. Fresh flowers display in a short space of time all the classic phases of life. Dried flowers are a suspension of life at one particular phase. They are separate entities. The sheen of the fresh petal has disappeared and the texture of the plant has changed, but their static beauty has charmed men and women for centuries.

In the early years of colonization of our continent, housewives gathered armfuls of Pearly Everlasting and Pussytoes and Goldenrod from the fields where they grew and dried and massed them in large bouquets to relieve the winter drabness of their homes. The women were following a tradition that was well established in the England they had left. There it had been the custom to bring a variety of Everlastings into the house in winter when flowers were scarce and place them about the rooms in vases and pots of sand. Chinese Lanterns (*Physalis Alkekengi*) decorated English rooms in the sixteenth century, and London flower markets of the early seventeenth century offered Strawflowers and Globe Amaranths often dyed vibrant colors, for home decoration. The names Strawflower, Immortelle, and Everlasting seem to have been used interchangeably (as they often are today) to describe any flower that had papery petals and the ability to retain its color and form indefinitely. Indeed some were observed to have an even more unusual attribute: When the flower head was dipped in water, it returned to the turgid state of the freshly picked flower. The texture of the flower changed back completely to what it had been before drying. Although the condition will last only until the petals dry again, it is interesting to see and it is a good way to reshape last year's Strawflowers.

Chinese Lanterns.

Hanging basket arrangement of Strawflowers and glycerinized Ivy.

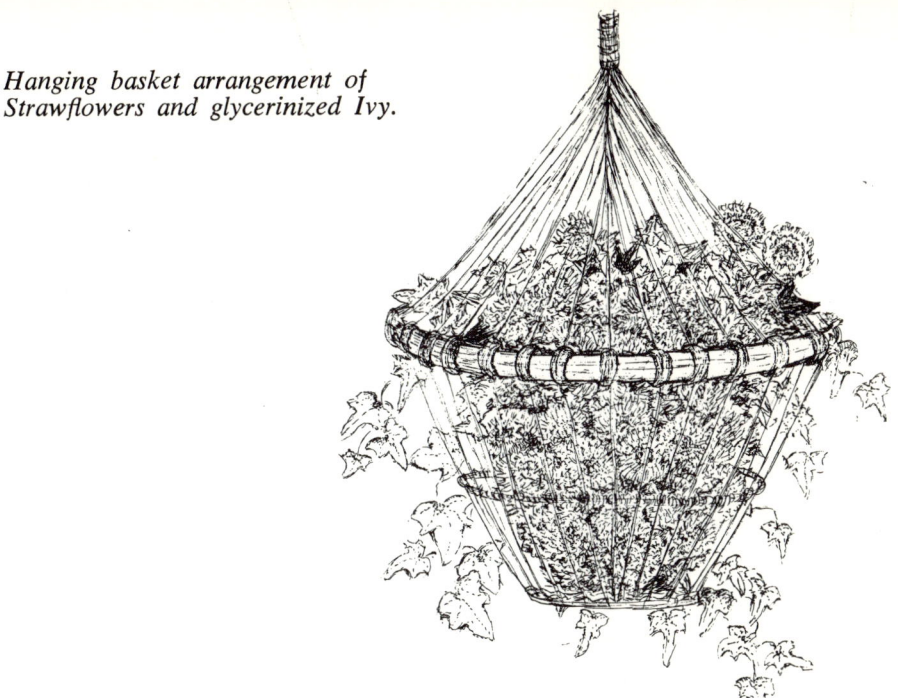

The first Strawflowers seem to have arrived in England as dried flowers at about the middle of the sixteenth century and they were cultivated there early in the seventeenth century. These were some species of Helichrysum, as well as the lovely Xeranthemum and Catananche called Cupid's-Dart, which in ancient times had been used to make a love potion. All of these flowers, as well as the Globe Amaranth, which was an ancient symbol of immortality, had their origins in Asia Minor and the Mediterranean countries. Centuries before, the Egyptians had used some of the same varieties in their funeral wreaths, and the Greeks and Romans had entwined them in wreaths and garlands to decorate their banquet tables. However, it is the far-off continent of Australia that has given us the greatest variety of Everlastings. *Helichrysum bracteatum* was the first Everlasting to be introduced into England from Australia, arriving there toward the end of the eighteenth century. This is the Strawflower that usually comes to mind when we use the term. Ammobium and two species of Helipterum often called Rhodanthe and Acroclinium are all of Australian origin but are now grown in other parts of the world and are easily cultivated here.

Strawflowers, Statice, Honesty pods, and many other readily dried flowers and pods enhanced interiors for hundreds of years, until the Victorians typically suffocated their naturalness in fussy overblown arrangements. After the Victorian period, dried materials lost favor for a while in home decoration. Today, their distinctive appearance and soft colors, displayed simply, seem appropriate to both modern and period interiors.

Sources of Flowers for Drying and Dried Flowers

The countryside and the garden are the best sources of flowers for drying or of flowers and pods already dried and waiting to be collected. In early springtime, diminutive wild flowers poke their heads through the remains of last fall, either in the woods or in the dormant grass of suburban lawns. These tiny pastel flower faces are delightful when pressed and framed in wild flower "prints." But the greatest harvest can be gathered from June until October. During these months, many wild and cultivated flowers can be collected in different stages of their growth for contrasts of color and texture. Some Hydrangeas change from green-white to blue to beige as the season progresses, and the flowers can be dried successfully at each stage. Goldenrod and Joe-Pye Weed are valuable decoratively when picked for drying in advanced bud, just before full bloom, and again in their faded fall colors, already dried on the stalk. Some plants begin producing pods during this season. Those with an early blooming period will have pods already dried on the stalk and ready for picking. There are many plants in addition to the well-known Honesty (*Lunaria*) and Chinese Lantern plant (*Physalis Alkekengi*) that produce interesting pods. Poppies, Hosta, and Morning Glories are just three of the many plants with interesting pods which are often overlooked.

In late autumn, after the first frost has cleared away some of the excess foliage, tall brown Mullein stalks dominate the countryside in many areas. These ancient plants were known to the soldiers of the Roman Empire who used the stalks, dipped in tallow, for torches. The stalk is the second-year growth of a biennial plant which produces a low-growing green rosette the first year. The rosette somewhat resembles a flower head and it can be dried successfully too. Dock and Teasel and Pearly Everlasting, as well as other regional wildings, stand in the autumn landscape already dried by nature, waiting for your taking.

If you are hardy enough, winter is a wonderful time to see the countryside in a new perspective and collect perhaps the most interesting dried materials. At this time, the successive frosts and winds and storms in most parts of the country have removed all but the most tenacious branches of pods and dry flower husks. Much of the material is contorted and the colors are the palest beiges and grays. Surprisingly, no matter how much you may have gathered from the same spot in the fall, the yield of new dried material is usually great and lovely.

If you lack the inclination or time to grow your own flowers for drying or to tramp around the natural world looking for them, florists and gift shops usually stock dried Strawflowers and tiny Starflowers, as well as dried pods, in the fall. In addition, all kinds of florist flowers, including Statice, Acacia (sometimes called florists' Mimosa) Violets, Roses, and some Orchids can be dried at home as long as they are fresh when processed. It's a good idea to determine when the flowers will be received at the florist's and to purchase and dry them immediately. Occasionally some florists offer more unusual dried plant materials, and mail order sources can supply interesting pods and even some Australian Everlastings not cultivated here. For greatest decorating variety, collecting from the garden, the countryside, and the florist should be a year-round activity.

Methods for Drying Flowers

Basically there are three ways to dry flowers: air drying, pressing, and drying in an agent, that is, burying the flowers in an absorbent preparation. In one way or another, all flowers can be dried. The method should be determined by the flower and the use for which it is intended. Flowers to be dried by any method and for any use should be picked in midmorning after the dew has evaporated and before the sun is high. Do not process wilted flowers, the results are worthless. If flowers wilt accidentally you can often revive them if you remove the foliage and place them in water up to the flower, heads for an hour or two. Weak-stemmed flowers such as violets and some small wild flowers can be revived by gently submerging them, flower and all, in water for a few minutes until they return to a turgid state. Foliage should be removed from the flower stem before drying by any method. If you want dried foliage, dry it at

Tool shed serves as a plant drying room.

the same time but separately. Good color retention in dried flowers depends upon the dryness and darkness of the drying environment. Dampness in the drying or storage area will cause mildew.

Air Drying

Air drying is the easiest and most natural way to dry flowers for winter bouquets. Just hang them in a warm dry dark room that has a circulation of air after the manner of herb drying in the monasteries of the middle ages. If you have a nice old-fashioned attic without windows or with windows that can be darkened, you have a perfect drying room. It will probably have space as well for storing the dried flowers and for bouquet making, which can be messy. Attics aren't too common any more, however, and other areas can be improvised: garages and sheds, for instance, or a closet with a louvered door in which lines can be strung or wire coat hangers hung and a shelf utilized for storage. Even a dim corner which can hold a wooden clothes drying rack will do. Our colonial ancestors probably hung flowers to dry by the fireplace along with the medicinal and pot herbs they dried for domestic use. In the small cabins with few if any windows, drying requirements could be met without thought.

Directions for Air Drying

Important: Strawflowers, those flowers with papery petals, must be picked in advanced (almost opened) bud. They will open as they dry. Those picked when opened will shatter when dried. Most other flowers dry best when picked just before the point of full bloom, but they may be dried at other stages as well.

Method

Materials needed: Wire twists or floral wire
Lines for hanging or a wooden drying rack or wire coat hangers

Environment: Dark, warm, and dry with air circulating

Note: Almost without exception basements, even when they seem dry, are too damp.

Procedure

Gather flowers in the morning.

Place stems in water immediately to prevent wilting.

Strip foliage from the plant stems.

Tie flower stems together with wire or Twistums: four or five medium-sized flowers to a bunch; ten or twelve small flowers to a bunch. Hang large flowers, such as Hydrangea, separately.

Tie the flowers to the line, drying rack, or clothes hanger.

Place so that the bunches of flowers do not touch.

Time for drying: Two or three weeks. Flowers will feel crisp.

When flowers are dry, spray each one thoroughly with a clear matte-finish plastic spray (usually available at art supply stores for spraying charcoal drawings).

Storage when dry

If space is not a consideration, the flowers can be left hanging after spraying until you are ready to use them. Otherwise place them in a cardboard box similar to a dress box or long floral box. Put tissue paper between layers of flowers. Place the box in an absolutely dry place such as a closet shelf.

Caution: Mice are attracted by dried flowers.

Some flowers to dry by hanging in air

These are just a few of the many flowers that can

be dried successfully by this method, so do experiment.

Acacia (Florists' Mimosa)
Baby's-Breath (*Gypsophila*)
Bells-of-Ireland
Butterfly Weed
Cattails—Spray lightly before hanging. Gather when Cattails first form, usually in June
Celosia
Chinese Lanterns
Clover flowers
Dock—Dry throughout the summer season
Globe Amaranth—Dry when fully opened
Goldenrod
Heather—Spray lightly before hanging, again when dry
Honesty (*Lunaria*)—Cut when pods begin to turn tan
Hydrangea—*H. paniculata grandiflora* dries well
Joe-Pye Weed and Boneset (varieties of the same plant)
Lavender flowers—Dry when one half opened
Mint flowers
Mullein stalk—The rosette should be dried in an agent
Pearly Everlasting (*Anaphalis margaritacea*)
Queen Anne's Lace (Wild Carrot)
Statice
Strawflowers
   Ammobium
   Catananche
   Helichrysum species
   Helipterum species including Rhodanthe and Acroclinium
   Xeranthemum
Yarrow

Some woody stemmed flowers can be air dried successfully if

they are placed in a jug containing a little water and allowed to remain until they are dry and crisp. The small amount of water will evaporate after a few days but it will keep the flowers from wilting before they start to dry. Color will be somewhat faded but still attractive. The ability of some wild flowers such as Goldenrod and Yarrow to dry easily may have been discovered accidentally in just this way.

Drying in an Agent

This method is especially useful for drying lovely single flowers. It preserves the form of the flower in a way that other methods cannot. Almost all flowers can be dried in an agent, although some colors will not dry satisfactorily. Experience will turn up the exceptions, but generally reds do not come true. Color retention in yellow and orange flowers can be breath-taking. As a rule only the flower head is dried in the agent and floral wire must replace the natural stem. Flowers dried in this way can be used in large winter bouquets but they seem most attractive when arranged in rather low bouquets with dried or glycerinized foliage (see Chapter Four) to hide the substitute stems. Corsages for sentimental keepsakes and flowers for three-dimensional craft projects such as shadow boxes and paperweights are most successfully dried by this method.

Four Different Agents

The drying agent will directly influence the results you can expect. Sand has been a favorite in the past, but its weight can distort the blooms. It must be sifted before using to remove any foreign paricles and it must be completely dry. Even so, it usually takes from ten days to three weeks for the flowers to dry, with a resulting color loss. A mixture of half corn meal and half borax can also be used as a drying agent. It must be thoroughly mixed so that the particles of borax and corn meal are evenly distributed throughout. This mixture is lighter than sand but it has a tendency to stick to the flower petals. Like sand it is influenced by atmospheric conditions. Flowers may dry in a week but usually take longer. Cat litter which is available under many commercial names is a good agent to use for drying large flowers and long-spike flowers.

It is light in weight and dries the flowers fairly quickly, in about a week or ten days. Some color loss can be expected. The most efficient drying agent is silica gel. It will dry flowers in from two to five days with resulting true-to-life color. It is lightweight so that no petal distortion results. The initial cost is high but it can be reused indefinitely. When the colored crystals turn pink the preparation can be heated in a 200-degree oven. After about fifteen minutes the crystals will turn blue and the agent can be used again. Silica gel is available at most garden centers and by mail order under the commercial name Flower Dri and it is recommended above all other agents for this method of drying flowers.

Successful drying of flowers in an agent is also dependent upon the way in which the flowers are placed. Directions will be given for three different shapes of flowers: spike flowers such as Delphiniums, flat flowers like Pansies or Shasta Daisies, and cup flowers like Tulips and Roses. Flowers to be dried in an agent may be dried in any stage of budding. They should be picked just before full bloom for drying as an opened flower.

Drying Flowers in an Agent
Materials needed
The agent of your choice
Container to hold the agent
For silica gel, a plastic refrigerator container with a cover is a good choice with masking tape to seal it
For other agents a shoe box or larger cardboard carton can be used
Small spoon
#20 floral wire
Wire-cutting shears
Plastic spray (matte finish)
Method
Pour the agent into the container to a depth of an inch.
Remove foliage from flowers.
For all flowers except spike flowers:
Cut off the flower stem, leaving about a quarter-

inch stub. Insert #20 floral wire up through calyx. Make a small hook. Draw hook gently down through calyx.

Cut wire stem to one inch.

Curve wire stem to the side.

To dry cup flowers such as Roses and Tulips:

Make a cuplike depression in the agent.

Place the flower, head up, in the depression.

With spoon and fingers gently sprinkle the agent around the outside of the flower until the bottom half is covered all around.

Now sprinkle the agent inside the flower and in between the petals of multiple-petaled flowers.

When the inside is filled to almost the same depth as the outside, start sprinkling the agent all around the outside again.

When the flower is completely surrounded by the agent, finish sprinkling additional agent inside.

With all flowers care should be taken not to damage the petal tips.

Finish by sprinkling a small amount of the agent back and forth over the top of the flower.

Stop when the flower is just covered.

To dry flat flowers such as Pansies and Daisies:

Make a slight depression in the agent.

Place the flower, head up, in the depression.

Starting at the outer edge of the petals, gently sprinkle the agent over the flower, following a circular pattern.

Stop when the flower is just covered.

To dry spike flowers such as Delphiniums:

Make a horizontal depression in the agent, wide enough to accommodate the flower.

Lay the flower in the depression.

Sprinkle the agent back and forth along either

side of the flower until both sides are covered.

Then sprinkle the agent over the top.

Stop when the flower is just covered.

You can dry as many flowers as you wish at one time as long as they do not touch each other in the container. It is best to dry similar flowers together so that the drying time will be the same.

Flowers drying in silica gel must be covered and the container sealed with masking tape. Flowers drying in other agents should be left uncovered and placed in a dark dry warm place.

Check flowers for dryness after the minimum time has passed.

Silica gel: two days

Other agents: one week

To do this, brush a little of the agent away from the flower and touch it gently. If it is dry it will feel crisp. If it does not, replace the agent and check again after a day or two, resealing the silica gel container each time. Continue checking until the flowers are completely dry.

Then, remove them carefully from the agent and spray with clear matte-finish plastic spray. Store the dried flowers in covered plastic containers or plastic bags which can be tied shut, and keep in a dark dry place until you are ready to arrange them. Directions for wiring stems to the flowers are given in the bouquet-making section of this chapter.

Pressing Flowers

If you have ever placed a flower between the pages of a book for a keepsake, you have pressed a flower but not in the best way. To press flowers so that they will have a high degree of color retention and good form, you must have an evenly weighted press that will absorb moisture rapidly. It's very easy to do, as the directions will show.

All kinds of flowers can be pressed, but large or small flowers with a single layer of petals like the Pansy are easiest. They may be pressed flat or in profile. Multiple-petaled flowers such as the Rose must be flattened gently with the fingers before being pressed, but results are not always satisfactory. Flowers similar to Tulips or Day Lilies are best pressed in profile. Flower foliage and extra stem lengths (helpful in "print" making) can be pressed at the same time as the flowers as long as they are separated from them by several layers of absorbent material (paper toweling). Flowers that are to be pressed fully opened should be picked just before the point of full bloom. Buds may be pressed at any stage.

Pressing Flowers

    Materials needed

        Two matching boards about 12" by 18". Pieces of masonite or plywood can be used

        A sheet of plastic about four times the size of the boards

        Wire twists to tie the plastic

        Roll of paper toweling

        Tin of silica gel crystals (Flower Dri)

    Note: Flowers have been pressed without silica gel for hundreds of years; however, it does speed the drying time, which results in greater color retention in the pressed flower. If you decide not to use silica gel, omit the plastic sheet and steps in procedure relating to it.

    Procedure

        Spread the plastic sheet on a flat surface such as a table top.

        Place one board in the center of the sheet.

        Place five thicknesses of paper toweling smoothly on the board.

        Remove foliage from the flowers.

        Cut stems short.

        Lay flower heads on the paper toweling, face down or in profile.

Smooth petals and straighten stems.
Do not permit material to touch or overlap.
Sprinkle lightly and evenly with silica gel.
Without disturbing the plant material cover it with one thickness of paper toweling.
Place four more layers of paper toweling over the first.
Dry as much plant material as you wish, sprinkling each layer with silica gel and separating each layer with five thicknesses of paper toweling.
Finish with five thicknesses of toweling.
Place the second board on top.
Draw up the corners of the plastic sheet and tie shut.
Weight the entire surface with bricks, boards, or heavy books.
Plant material must process in a dry area.
Check for dryness, after two days, if using silica gel; after a week, if not. The plant material should feel crisp.
Leave in the press until completely dry.
Store pressed plant material in wax sandwich bags or stamp collectors' envelopes in a dark dry place.

How to Make a Flower "Print"

Pressed flowers are useful for many craft projects but are most attractive decoratively when used in framed flower prints. These are not difficult to make but they do take patience. The dried materials can be remarkably perverse, shifting just when your design seems complete. Glue frequently discolors plant material after a few months and should not be used to hold it in place.

A flower print can be large or small. It can follow an eighteenth-century design with old-fashioned garden flowers, or it can be a sampling of local wild flowers, simply arranged. Modern designs are especially handsome.

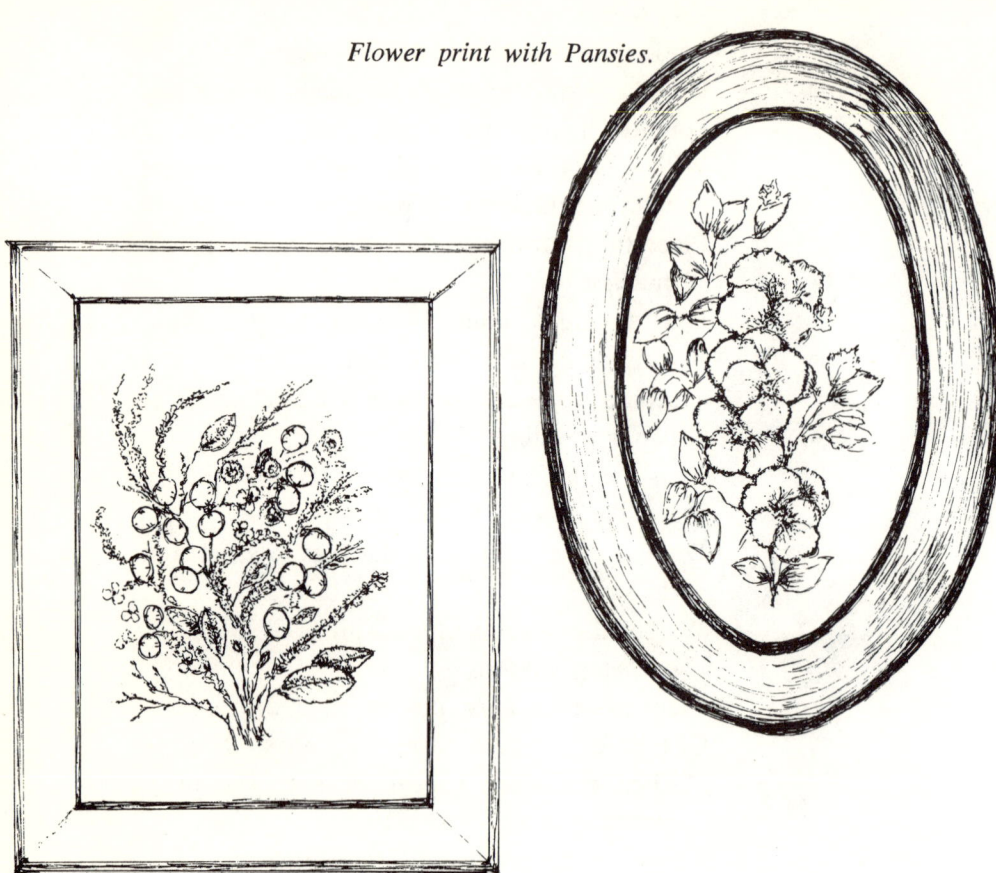

Flower print with Pansies.

Flower print with dried flowers and pods.

To Make a Flower Print
Materials needed

    Picture frame of your choice with glass
    The picture backing
    The background, slightly larger than the backing. This can be construction or drawing paper or cloth such as burlap or linen or shantung, etc.
    Wedges of heavy cardboard to push the backing against the glass

Tape to secure the print in the frame and make it airtight

Procedure

Have flowers and foliage ready.

Lay the background on the picture backing.

Square off corners and fold the background material over the picture backing.

Secure in place with glue or staples.

Tentatively place the flowers on the background, following an old-fashioned print or a sketch or your imagination.

Let some flowers overlap to add depth to the design. Separate stems and foliage allow flexibility. If you are working with very small plant materials tweezers can be helpful in moving them about.

When you are pleased with your design:

Be sure picture frame is lying back side up on your work table.

Lower the glass carefully over the plant material. Line up the bottom of the glass with the bottom of the backing, then lower the top of the glass into place.

Now move the whole unit toward the edge of your work table until a little more than half extends over the edge. Take hold of this part, firmly placing the four fingers of each hand on the underside and the two thumbs, pressing down, on top.

With a quick twist of your wrist turn the picture over and place it in the frame.

Fasten the print in place.

Push wedges underneath the sides of the frame.

Seal all around the back edge with masking tape.

Framed flower prints are long-lasting accessories, but direct sunlight will fade the flower colors, so take care where you hang them.

Colonial bouquet arranged by Miss Edna Pennell for Colonial Williamsburg.

Arranging and Placing Dried Bouquets

Flower prints can be made or hung at any time of the year, but October, with the first hint of winter in the air, seems to be the time to make dried bouquets. If you have the previously mentioned attic, this is the place to do it. Dried materials grab and cling to each other and anything that's close with a resulting shower of stems, petals, and leaves. A drop cloth is a help.

Flowers that have been dried in an agent will need longer stems before they can be used in most bouquets. In addition, the stems of many Strawflowers are too weak to support the flower head and may have to be replaced with wire stems. To add a long stem to agent-dried flowers, just take a length of ※20 floral wire and twist it once tightly around the stub stem you placed in the flower head before putting it in the agent. After one twist straighten the long wire so that it is parallel to the wire stub. Now take brown or green floral tape and, starting at the top under the flower head, wind it around and down the wire stem until the stem is covered. The stems can be cut easily with wire clippers to suit the height of a particular arrangement. They can be lengthened again as easily. Just tape another length of floral wire to the first stem.

To give Strawflowers and other weak-stemmed, air-dried flowers new stems, push a length of ※20 floral wire gently up through the calyx (the center of the flower). Pull the wire up far enough to make a tiny hook, and then gently, holding the bottom of the wire, pull the hook down into the calyx. Do this carefully so that you don't break the flower head. Then cover the stem, as above, with floral tape.

Almost anything that is appropriate to your home and the plant material can be used to hold a dried bouquet. Since water is not needed you can improvise containers from baskets, jugs, pitchers, boxes, and almost anything that comes to mind. Often the con-

Wiring Strawflowers.

tainer will suggest a bouquet. An antique boughpot is attractive with an overflowing mass of one kind dried material such as Goldenrod or Boneset, perhaps placed on the floor beside an open door in an early American period family room. A stoneware jug with just a few stalks of Queen Anne's Lace or Cattails might go beside the fireplace in a contemporary room, or a starkly modern room, as well as in a more rustic interior. The clean simple lines of the plant materials would be at home anywhere, the jug would necessarily indicate informal surroundings. A pewter pitcher may suggest Hydrangeas dried in palest beige and placed on a highly polished sideboard in a dining room. Colonial ladies made large mixed bouquets of both wild and cultivated Everlastings. These bouquets followed as many patterns as there were ladies, for there were no limiting rules. The results ranged from homespun to elegant. If this sort of bouquet seems difficult to arrange, a basic pattern may help. You can follow it to make bouquets of any size, from miniature to huge.

Decide first where the arrangement will be displayed, then choose your container. If you wish, fill it three fourths full of moist sand. Actually a full bouquet will support itself but the sand is helpful while you are arranging the material and provides stabilizing weight when the bouquet is displayed. You will need three forms of dried material: If you are arranging a large bouquet, spikes such as Mullein or Cattails, airy filler such as Statice or Baby's-Breath, and well-defined flower heads such as Strawflowers will be in scale. To start, place a stalk of Mullein straight up in the very center of the vase. It should be about twice the height of the vase. You can, if you wish, measure it roughly by holding it upside down next to the vase. At either side of the first stalk of Mullein place additional stalks, in gradually declining heights, following a fanlike pattern. Add the Baby's-Breath (filler) on either side and all around the stalks. Place four or five Strawflowers close together in the center of the bouquet at the rim of the vase. Gradually add more Strawflowers further apart and rising in the bouquet. Look for open spaces and add filler material so that the finished bouquet has a full overflowing appearance. Use this pattern as a beginning but don't let it stifle your own ideas. It can be varied infinitely. Dried leaves

Colonial bouquet.

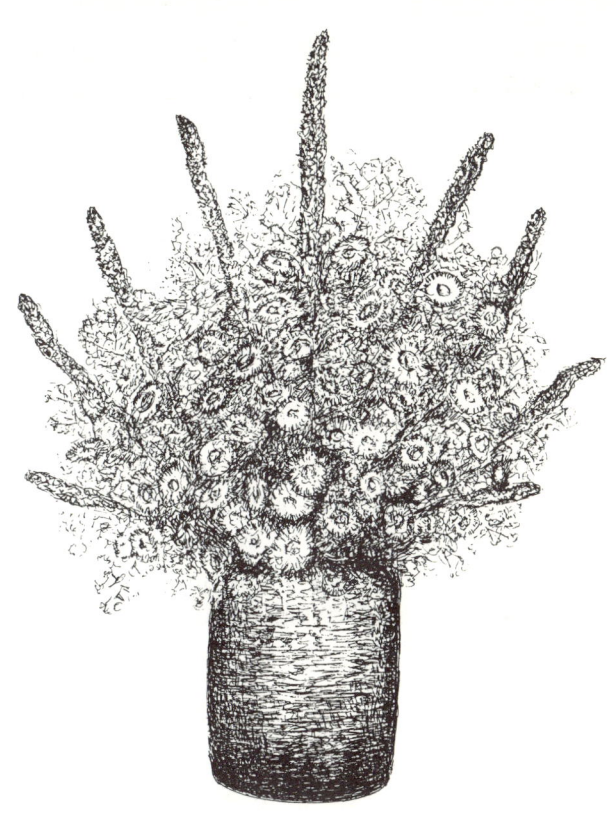

or Fern (see Chapter Four) or Celosia plumes can replace the spike or filler material. Any well-defined flower head can be used for the Strawflowers.

Dried materials can be arranged with fresh flowers or foliage, and the result is an intriguing study in contrasts. The Japanese often do this in delightfully simple arrangements that seem at home in any interior. Five medium-sized Chrysanthemums with their stems cut short at slightly varying lengths are lovely with perhaps a dozen twisted stemmed Poppy pods. A narrow jar-shaped container about six inches high would be most appropriate to hold the arrangement. Place a small piece of crumpled wire in the bottom to hold the plant material or, for greater stabilization, stuff the vase with water-soaked Oasis. The water won't damage the dried material during the limited life of the arrangement.

A hanging basketry birdcage filled with Strawflowers and curves of glycerinized Ivy (see Chapter Four) will bring color and movement to perhaps an otherwise drab kitchen that may be too small for most floral accents. Hung from the ceiling over a breakfast bar, it takes no space but adds immeasurably to the warmth and charm of the room.

Flowers dried in an agent can be arranged in small rounded bouquets and placed about the house, wherever a decorative accent is needed. The bouquets are easily arranged. Just anchor a round Styrofoam form to the floor of a low round container with floral clay. Cut the wire stems to varying short lengths and poke them into the Styrofoam, so that the flower heads are close together but not touching. Fill in the arrangement with sprigs of dried foliage (see Chapter Four). An opened antique box filled with dried flowers is an attractive desk accessory. You can make it in much the same way as the small scatter bouquets, using a block of Styrofoam anchored inside the box to hold the flowers. The arrangement should have an appearance of overflowing abundance.

Miniatures

Miniature dried bouquets can be made in a variety of ways. Containers can be improvised or the miniature vases mentioned in the chapter on fresh flowers can be used. Dried material can be held in place with sand or pieces of Styrofoam stuffed into the tall vases. A tiny piece of clay will hold the flowers in a shallow container. You can make a miniature colonial bouquet following the basic pattern suggested above. Use Mint flowers for the spike form, dried immature Ferns or Herb leaves (see Chapter Four) for filler, and single twigs of Baby's-Breath or Boneset for flower heads. The effect is enchanting. You can make a Victorian domed arrangement easily. Shape a miniature cone from a piece of Styrofoam, using a razor blade. Anchor this to the separate base of the dome with floral clay. Use tiny dried flowers that have been dried in an agent, poking their short wire stem stubs into the miniature cone until the cone is covered. Fill in between the flowers with tips of dried foliage. Cover with the dome. This is an engaging accessory for a writing table or desk. A mail order source for domes is listed in Chapter Ten.

A miniature open bouquet with an oriental feeling can be made using a twig of dried Morning Glory pods and several single dried Starflowers. Anchor a piece of clay to the floor of a small glass coaster and place the stalks of pods first. Cut the stems of several Starflowers short and place these so that the clay is concealed. A whimsical accent for a hanging corner shelf.

Domed miniature bouquet.

Gifts

The most attractive gifts can be made from dried flowers. Because you make them yourself using natural materials they are unique and seem to carry with them an extra dimension of thoughtfulness. For a friend who is ill, a lasting bouquet of Strawflowers and sprigs of dried Rosemary foliage, arranged in a milk-glass basket, makes a colorful and fragrant remembrance—one that can be enjoyed long after the illness is forgotten. It's easy to arrange, if you anchor a rounded Styrofoam form to the floor of the basket with floral clay. Then just poke the shortened stems of the Strawflowers into the Styrofoam until it is fairly well covered. Tuck in fragrant dried sprigs of herb foliage and add perhaps a white ribbon, low on one side of the basket handle, for a dressed up appearance.

Of course, attractively framed flower prints are always welcomed. These need only to be boxed and gift wrapped and are especially charming as welcoming gifts to a neighborhood newcomer. The Victorian dome arrangement described in the section on miniatures, above, can be made in any size and is handsome

Dried wild flowers sparsely arranged in a floor-standing bouquet.

76 DRIED FLOWERS AND PODS

Dried Mullein in a floor-standing container complements the other accessories decorating this rustic fireplace.

enough for a birthday or other special-occasion gift. Like the print, it needs only to be boxed and gift wrapped and sent on its way.

A bouquet of delicate air-dried materials that are difficult to find in the shops is a delightful casual gift to give when none is really expected. Silvery Honesty pods or Chinese Lanterns are especially appropriate made up in good-sized hand bouquets with

DRIED FLOWERS AND PODS

the stems wrapped in tissue paper or green florist's paper so that the recipient can rearrange them in her own favorite vase.

Dried flowers and pods can be enjoyed in so many decorative ways. As you work with them, you will find your imagination stimulated by the form and color and texture of the materials. What you see and what you feel about the materials will help you create bouquets and decorative accessories that are uniquely your own.

Mail Order Sources:

Floral Art P. O. Box 394, Highland Sta. Springfield, Mass. 01109	*Dried flowers and pods. Arranging equipment. Catalogue.*
Garden Club Products Mapes' Garden Center Route 1, Kennebunk, Me. 04043	*Dried pods. Flower Dri kit. Catalogue.*
Williamsburg Craft Center Colonial Williamsburg, Inc. Williamsburg, Va. 23185	*Boxes of dried flowers. Catalogue.*
Stephen Barany 149 E. 72nd St. New York, N.Y. 10021	*Dried Australian wild flowers. No catalogue.*
The Pod Happy Shop 865 Third St. St. Petersburg, Fla. 33704	*Dried pods and other interesting dried materials.*
Boycan's Floral Arts 1052 E. State St. Sharon, Penna. 16146	*A wealth of dried materials including pods, dried Strawflowers, and dried Starflowers. Catalogue.*

Chapter Four

Foliage

Foliage is the most versatile and varied of all the natural plant materials. The supple leaves of the Lilies, the lacelike Ferns, the sturdy grasses and curving vines and the broad leaves and needles of trees and shrubs all have decorating possibilities. One tree can often provide foliage in colors that vary from the pale greens of springtime to the blazing reds of fall. Its leaves can be air dried or pressed or glycerinized to make them permanent. Its branches can be forced into bloom or leaf indoors while the world is still bare outside. For most of the year it can add living color to dim areas, where nothing else will survive.

Foliage has been used decoratively for thousands of years. Garlands and wreaths of Ivy and Grape leaves graced the banquet tables of ancient Egypt. Wheat was tied together in stylized sheaves for religious offerings. The Romans made decorative garlands of Thyme and Mint and Dill and Fern, often intertwined with flowers chosen for their symbolic meanings. The intricate outlines of individual leaves were seen and appreciated. The beauty of the Acanthus leaf was made permanent in the stone of the Corinthian column. Much later, the great medieval cathedrals were embellished with stone carvings of Ivy and Fern, executed with the clarity and skill that comes from intent observation. The leaf motif was woven into tapestries and appeared in the borders of the illuminated manuscripts of the Middle Ages.

In Japan branches of foliage in aesthetic arrangement have been enjoyed for centuries. The classical rikka style combined many different branches of interesting line in complicated arrangements that symbolized woodland scenes. The Pine tree was a masculine symbol of long life. Pine branches are still combined with the Rose in Japanese flower arrangements to contrast masculine strength with feminine frailty. Some of the most appealing Japanese arrangements have branches of leafy foliage carefully pruned to bring out their best line and then arranged with flowers to decorate the tokonoma alcove of the Japanese home. The same arrangement can be easily adapted to American homes. It would be lovely on a chest in a formal living room, for instance, if a tall container compatible with the other furnishings were used. A piece of crumpled wire placed in the container will hold the branch ends in place. Directions for conditioning the branches are given later in this chapter.

Sparse oriental arrangement of branches and flowers.

In our own country, our colonial ancestors gathered autumn leaves and pressed them for winter ornament. In summer they placed boughpots overflowing with leafy branches in their empty fireplaces, continuing the custom of the England they had left—a custom that is equally attractive in today's fireplaces.

Casual foliage arrangement.

Sources of Foliage for Decorating

Foliage of one kind or another is so easy to obtain that it can provide decorative accents in your home all through the year. The florist is one excellent source. Eucalyptus which is hardy only in some areas of California and Florida is available through florists in most parts of the country, usually plentiful in January and February. This exotic foliage is extremely long lasting when fresh, and it can be glycerinized and pressed successfully. Incidentally it retains its intriguing fragrance after processing. Shallon, sometimes called Lemon Leaf, and Pittosporum have the same long-lasting quality and ability to press and absorb glycerine. Huckleberry is long lasting but does not process very well for permanent use. Asparagus Fern will last only a day or two when fresh but it will retain its color for a season when pressed. It is especially attractive in winter bouquets. In addition to the usual florist foliages mentioned above, some florists will have Magnolia and Rhododendron foliages and local foliages in season. Pussy Willows in early spring are fairly standard.

In the fall treated autumn leaves such as Oak or Maple are available at many florists. Some will stock dried Wheat or Barley and Pampas Grass as well. Mail order sources can provide fresh needled Evergreen foliage in the late fall, as well as some dried or processed foliages and grasses at any time of the year.

The garden or countryside can provide branches of foliage from shrubs or trees, and woody vines, for pressing or glycerinizing or for immediate use. Branches can be gathered in late winter for forcing either the leaves or the flowers. Single leaves of medium texture like Galax can be cut from indoor or outdoor plants for long-lasting fresh effects or for pressing or glycerinizing. Wild and cultivated grasses and strap leaves are attractive fresh or dried. When you gather foliage, consider the parent plant. Use wire cutters or sharp pruning shears to make clean cuts from the bottom or sides of the plant. Long branches of foliage will keep crisp if you wrap them in wet newspapers as soon as they are cut. Place Ferns and grasses and smaller stems of foliage in wet paper toweling in a plastic bag to prevent wilting. Approach foliage gathering in an experimental mood and the results can be pleasantly surprising. In a short while, you may find certain trees and plants emerging from the anonymous blend of the landscape and becoming familiar.

At the end of this chapter, a chart lists many popular foliages with their probable length of cut life and the methods by which they can be preserved.

Conditioning Fresh Foliage

All fresh foliage will last longer if it is properly conditioned. Look for mature woody stemmed growth on shrubs and trees. New springtime shoots do not have a long cut life. If you are collecting Ivy, choose some stems that are climbing upward and others that curve down for flexibility in decorating.

To Condition Fresh Foliage from Countryside, Florist, or Garden:

  Dip dusty or muddy foliage in soapy water, swish around, and then rinse in clear water.

  Submerge all foliage for at least an hour in cold water.

  Remove branched foliage of trees and shrubs after one hour.

   Take each branch and remove damaged leaves, old twigs, and unwanted cross stems.

   Crush about three inches of the branch ends with a hammer.

   Rinse the branch ends under fast-running water to remove woody particles.

   Place upright in deep water for several hours or overnight, then arrange.

  Remove strap leaves, vines, grasses, and small stems of foliage and single leaves after one hour's submersion in water and arrange.

  Needled Evergreens should be left overnight in the cold-water bath.

  Ferns other than florists' Asparagus Fern should be submerged in water for four or five hours.

  Do not condition Asparagus Fern. Place it in the vegetable crisper if you cannot use it right away.

Conditioned foliage will usually last longer if you add a commercial cut-flower preservative such as Floralife to the water in which it is displayed. This will keep the water sweet as well. If you don't use a preservative, do put a piece of charcoal in the container to keep the water fresh. Use as much water as your container will hold. Remove any foliage below the water level and keep the level constant with additions of fresh water.

Conditioning Flowering Branches

Flowering branches from trees and shrubs can be used for delightful decorating effects. Gather them when the buds of the flowers are about three quarters open. Crush about three inches of the stem end with a hammer and rinse the crushed stem end under fast-running water. Condition the branches overnight in deep water in a cool dim place. Be sure the blossoms are above the water level. Spray unopened buds with a fine mist of water after the branches are arranged. Add commercial flower preservative to the water in which they are arranged. Flowering branches in oversized arrangements can bring springtime right into your home. Choose an appropriate tall container, add a stone or other weight to stabilize it, and perhaps a piece of crumpled floral wire to catch the stems and place the arrangement where it will affect the entire room with is freshness and beauty.

Oversized arrangement of flowering branches.

Forcing Branches

You can have a lovely preview of spring in your home with winter-forced branches. Both flowering and non-flowering branches are interesting to observe. Soft new green leaves are as beautiful in their own way as the more spectacular blossoms of flowering branches. Branches for forcing should be pruned from trees or shrubs on a mild winter day about four or five weeks before the normal blooming or leafing time. The buds which were set last fall or summer should have begun to swell. Remember to experiment. Bring in any branch with swelling buds even if you don't recognize it. The results can be intriguing. But if you want more certain results, here is a list of branches that force fairly easily:

Apple	Pear
Beech	Plum
Cherry	Pussy Willow
Dogwood	Quince
Forsythia	Redbud
Maple	Spicebush
Oak	Spirea

To force cultivated or wild branches:

> Choose branches at least a quarter inch thick and two feet long for best results.
> Remove damaged leaves and twigs.
> Crush three inches of the branch ends.
> Rinse the ends under fast-running water.
> Submerge horizontally in warm water for two or three hours.
> Then place in deep containers of cold water.
> Add a piece of charcoal to keep the water sweet.
> Change water weekly, recutting stems and crushing stem ends as necessary.
> Spray buds with a fine mist of water several times weekly.

The branches force best in a temperature of about 68 degrees. They need light but must be kept out of direct sun. When the blos-

Bare branches ready to leaf add dramatic interest to an empty corner.

88 FOLIAGE

soms or leaves begin to open, move the container into the sunlight to intensify the colors. You can watch the branches come into bloom in your living room if it is not too warm. Blooming or leafing usually takes several weeks, depending on the type of branch and the development of the buds.

Tall arrangement of Pussy Willows brings drama to an informal room. (Sand inside the container adds height to the branches.)

Preserving Foliage in Glycerine

Many single leaves, vines, and branches of foliage can be preserved permanently with a solution of glycerine and water. The leaves remain pliable and change to colors that range from dark green through bronze to chocolate brown, depending upon the time of year and the type of leaf you are processing. Generally all foliage will process most successfully during the months of June through September. You can process foliage at other times of the year but expect varying results. The foliage chart at the end of the chapter lists a number of leaves that can be glycerinized, but do experiment. Usually any fairly heavy leaf is worth trying either singly or as part of a branch. Glycerinized foliage can be arranged with or without water.

To Glycerinize Foliage:

Process in a dry area away from sunlight.
Do not try to process wilted foliage.
Remove damaged leaves and odd twigs.

Wall-hung arrangement of glycerinized foliage.

Rinse dusty leaves under running water or dip in suds and rinse.

To process branched foliage such as Magnolia or Beech

Note: Branches should not exceed twenty inches in length.

Materials needed

Glycerine (from the druggist)—a half pint is usually enough at first

Pint jar such as a mayonnaise jar

Water

Procedure

Crush stem ends with a hammer.

Rinse crushed ends under fast-running water.

Make a solution of one part glycerine to two parts water.

Pour solution in the jar to a depth of six inches.

Place the stem ends of one or two branches of foliage in the solution.

Do not crowd. There should be a circulation of air around the leaves.

Remove the branches when the solution reaches the tips of the leaves.

(The leaves will have changed color gradually)

Time for processing: one to three weeks or longer.

Note: Foliage can be enjoyed decoratively as it processes; just place the jar of solution inside an attractive container.

To Process Single Leaves and Vines:

Materials needed

Glycerine

Water

Oblong container such as a plastic refrigerator carton

Procedure
>Make a solution of one part water to one part glycerine.
>Fill container to a depth of about three inches.
>Submerge leaves or vines in the solution.
>If necessary, weight the leaves with a stone or other heavy object to keep them submerged.
>Check frequently; the leaves will change color when absorption is complete.
>Remove and store or arrange.
>Time for processing: five days to two weeks, seldom longer.
>Storage: Store glycerinized foliage between tissue paper in cardboard boxes in a dry place. Dampness can cause the foliage to mildew.

Store the remaining glycerine solution in a covered jar and it can be reused indefinitely. Despite the dramatic change in the foliage, only a small amount of the solution is absorbed during processing.

Press Drying Branches of Green or Autumn Foliage

Large branches of leaves can be preserved in their natural colors, for a season or two, if they are pressed. The procedure is much the same as that followed for pressing flowers, although the size of the branches necessitates a few changes. The leaves may be dried at any stage of their development, from springtime green to the lovely colors of autumn. Gather autumn leaves when their color has just reached its peak. The sap should still be running in the branch. If they are gathered too late, the leaves will fall from the branches after they are dried. If gathered too early, the color will not be as lovely. Do not press wilted leaves. When you collect foliage for pressing follow the general directions given earlier for collecting fresh foliage. Take along either wet newspapers or a pail of water to keep the leaves fresh. The leaves should be pressed in the same dark dry area required for drying flowers. If the frequently mentioned attic is not available, perhaps a closet shelf or even the space beneath a bed can be used. The leaves must press undisturbed for from three to six weeks.

To Press Large Branches of Leaves Including Autumn Leaves:
>*Materials needed*
>>A good pile of newspapers
>>Weights such as a large piece of masonite or several planks
>
>*Procedure*
>>Rinse dusty or muddy leaves in water and let the leaves air dry before pressing.
>>Prune away damaged leaves and any cross twigs or branches.
>>Place five layers of newspaper where the leaves are to be pressed.
>>Place a branch of leaves face down on the newspapers.
>>The branch must lie flat.
>>All leaves must be on the newspaper.
>>Smooth each leaf.
>
>Be sure no leaves are overlapping or touching.
>>Dry as many branches as you wish, just separate each branch of leaves with five layers of newspaper.
>>Place weights evenly over the top of the last five layers of newspaper.
>>Check the leaves after three weeks.
>>Leaves will feel crisp if dry. If the leaves are not thoroughly dry they will wilt, so if you are in doubt leave them a little longer. They may remain in the papers for several months without loss of color.
>>Spray dried leaves with a clear matte-finish plastic spray available at art stores for spraying charcoal drawings.
>>Store carefully in a dry place.

Drying Other Types of Foliage

Grains, grasses, single leaves, Ferns, and short stems of herb and other plant foliages can be pressed as flowers are pressed. Follow the directions given in Chapter Three, including sprinkling each layer of foliage with silica-gel crystals. In addition, grasses and grains and some herb foliages can be dried by hanging in air in the same manner as flowers. See Chapter Three for directions for air drying. Grains should be sprayed with a clear matte-finish plastic spray after drying by either method.

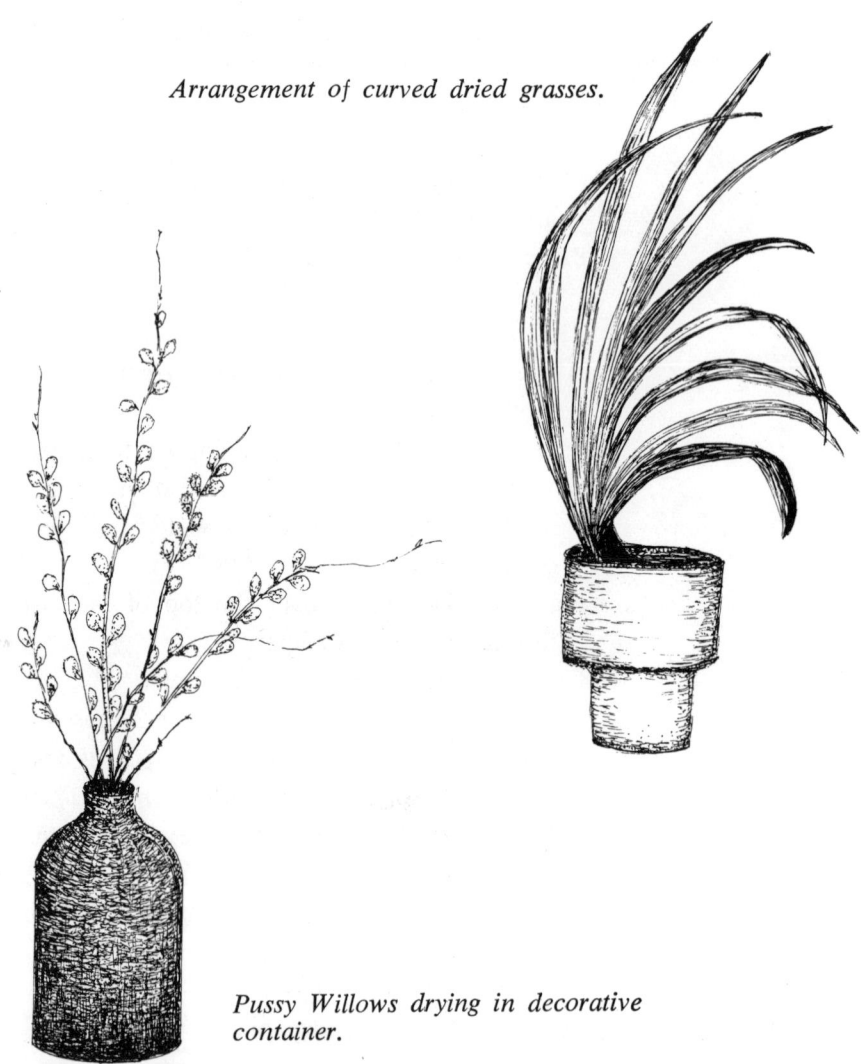

Arrangement of curved dried grasses.

Pussy Willows drying in decorative container.

Pussy Willows should be gathered in early spring, when the catkins are half opened. They can be hung to dry or they can be placed in a decorative container without water and allowed to dry right in your living room. Just keep them out of sunlight. Spray Pussy Willows with a clear matte-finish plastic spray when dry.

Decorating with Foliage

Foliage is a basic decorating accessory. How you use it will depend upon your own home and your own reaction to the line and texture and the subtle gradations of color of leaves and branches. Used generously, in all its variety, at all seasons, it can contribute warmth and charm to any home. It will form an attractive background and combine well with all the other natural materials: fresh and dried flowers, fruits and vegetables, driftwood and pine cones and pods. Alone it can make an important decorating statement. It can fill empty corners and add a finishing touch to sparsely furnished rooms. When flowers are scarce, foliage can be used instead and with more simplicity and naturalness. Especially when entertaining, foliage can add to the festive appearance of your home without budget strain. Florist foliages are always a bargain. And garden foliage whether long lasting or not can be pressed into decorative service for an evening with striking results. All foliage looks its best in simple natural arrangements. Generally foliage bouquets need no holders, but a small piece of crumpled chicken wire can be placed in the bottom of the container to catch the stems and provide stability, if you wish. Pressed leaves, because they are flat, should be placed so that some branches face to the sides and others to the front for an illusion of depth.

Glycerinized leaves can be used for permanent decorating accents. Several curving vines of glycerinized Ivy can be arranged in matching wall vases in a long narrow hall that might otherwise be difficult to decorate. A lavish bouquet of glycerinized Magnolia or Rhododendron leaves on a chest perhaps in front of a mirror that will magnify its shining impact is a handsome accessory for any formal area.

If you have a space that calls for a large permanent accessory, try a floor-standing container of long branched foliage that can

A handsome silver bowl holds a Christmas arrangement of garden foliage accented with tiny ornaments.

be changed with the season. In winter enjoy a generous bouquet of needled Evergreen branches. Add branches being forced, to the needled Evergreens, in late winter. In springtime arrange some flowering branches, with broad-leafed greens that have been pruned somewhat to eliminate any impression of jungle growth. In summer use a variety of shrubbery foliage with an emphasis on variations of cool green. In fall arrange glycerinized leaves with perhaps some dried Strawflowers followed by an abundant display of pressed autumn leaves.

A few stalks of grains or grasses, dried or fresh, curving gracefully from the narrow neck of a jug is an understated accessory that can, with the choice of the jug, complement almost any interior. Pussy Willow or Eucalyptus are attractive arranged in the same way. A table bouquet of leafy branches, judiciously

Aucuba foliage in a large glass container that is just right for this handsome chest.

pruned, can create a lovely airy effect, casting interesting shadows in sunlight or lamplight or candlelight. It can be used most appropriately for a centerpiece when unexpected dinner guests appear.

Scatter small and miniature bouquets of herb or plant foliage all through the house, in the bathroom, on night tables, desks, anywhere and everywhere. Improvise containers from baskets (with a jar inside to hold water) to teapots. The effect is delightful. Glycerinized or dried foliage can be used in these same bouquets for permanent effects with less care.

Small scatter bouquet of mixed foliage.

Cut Life and Preserving Techniques for Foliage

The following list contains the names of some of the better known foliages with the approximate minimum length of time they will last after cutting and conditioning as well as the preserving processes that can be used most successfully. Most of the foliages are long lasting. The list is small indication of the many kinds of foliage available. Do experiment with those not included.

Legend: P—*pressing*
                     G—*glycerinizing*
                     I—*indefinitely*
                     R—*may root*
                     H—*hanging*

FOLIAGE	DAYS OF CUT LIFE	METHOD OF PRESERVATION
Trees		
Bamboo	10	P
Beech	25	P, G
Dogwood	20	P, G
Evergreens, Needled	15	
(Length of cut life will vary with variety)		
Magnolia	20	P, G
Maple	15	P, G
Oak	15	P, G
Sweet Gum	10	P, G
Shrubs and Vines		
Aucuba	I, R	P, G
Dusty Miller	5	P, H
Evergreens, Needled	7	
Grape Ivy	20	P
Holly	10	
Ivy	I, R	P, G
Laurel	15	P, G
Privet	7	
Rhododendron	I	P, G
Scotch Broom	15	P, G, H
Long-lasting Florist Foliage		
Asparagus Fern	3	P
Eucalyptus	I	P, G
Galax	I	P, G
Huckleberry	20	
Pittosporum	20	P, G
Salal (Lemon Leaf)	20	P, G
Wild and Cultivated Grasses and Grains	7	P, H
Strap Leaves		
Calla	10	P, H
Canna	10	P, H
Gladiola	5	P, H
Iris	5	P, H

FOLIAGE	DAYS OF CUT LIFE	METHOD OF PRESERVATION
Ferns in Variety	4	P

Long-lasting herb foliages; expect about 20 days' cut life. Foliage can be dried by pressing or hanging.

        Basil   Rosemary
        Marjoram Sage
        Mint   Thyme
        Parsley

Long-lasting houseplant foliage. Expect about 15 days' cut life; however, many will root. Leaves can be dried by pressing.

        Aspidistra will last indefinitely
        Caladium
        Coleus
        Philodendron
        Sansevieria
        Sprengeri
        Wandering Jew

Mail Order Sources:

The Pod Happy Shop
865 Third St.
St. Petersburg, Fla. 33704

Dried grasses.

Clarendon Gardens Nursery
Pinehurst, N.C. 28374

Interesting fresh foliage.

Floral Art
P. O. Box 394, Highland Sta.
Springfield, Mass. 01109

Dried and glycerinized foliage. Catalogue.

Boycan's Floral Arts
1052 E. State St.
Sharon, Penna. 16146

Dried materials. Grasses. Grains. Glycerinized foliage. Catalogue.

Putney Nursery
Putney, Vt. 05346

Fresh evergreen foliage. Brochure.

Chapter Five

Houseplants

Houseplants are alive, quite obviously, but that is their charm. The beauty of other natural materials is either static or, like cut flowers, declining as we enjoy it. Houseplants are a constantly changing, living sample of the natural world that we can enjoy in our own homes. If we mistreat them, they sulk, and if we continue to neglect them they wither and die. But given good care and some understanding, they flourish, putting out new shoots and leaves with lusty abandon.

Most popular houseplants come from exotic corners of the world, Africa, Asia, Central and South America; places where the climate is tropical and sub-tropical. Some grow into tall shrubs and trees in their native soil. Many are able to adjust to our homes by curtailing their growth. Other plants need so much pampering that only the hobbyist willing to spend much time and effort can bring them to perfection. For decorative purposes, we need hardy plants that can be placed where their size and texture will add interest to an interior. Window gardens are delightful but we must have plants that will survive without sunlight as well.

They should thrive when given reasonable care, and a little neglect should not cause disaster. There is a host of plants with these easy-going traits, including vines and tall floor standing varieties, as well as miniatures and table-top sizes. The list at the end of this chapter offers a selection of easily cultivated plants that are suitable for many decorative uses.

When you have selected a plant and brought it into your home, give it several days to adjust to its new environment. Keep it away from strong sunlight and don't be concerned if it drops a few leaves. It will soon take hold.

General Houseplant Culture

Watering

Too much water will cause the roots of your houseplants to rot; too little water and they will shrivel. Flowering plants when in bud and flower require more water than foliage plants. It's a great puzzle to know how much water is enough for a particular plant. The United States Department of Agriculture, in its House & Garden Bulletin No. 133—Indoor Gardens for Decorative Plants, recommends a fail-safe method for watering houseplants that I enthusiastically pass on to anyone who will listen. To follow their method you will need a small plastic funnel. Place the neck of the funnel into the soil in the pot. Fill the funnel with water and when it empties, fill it again as often as necessary. When water no longer drains from the funnel, poke your finger down inside to prevent any remaining water from draining out and remove the funnel. I use a large funnel for floor standing plants and a small one for other plants, and I let my houseplants become almost dry before rewatering.

Humidity

Most houseplants need a humid atmosphere if they are to flourish. You can provide this easily if you place them in their pots on a layer of moist pebbles or stones. Small white stones from the garden center or chips from the aquarium supply store are fine. If you are using a decorative outer pot, place the pebbles inside, add water, and put the plant in its clay pot on top of the pebbles. The water should not touch the bottom of the pot. Pour additional water over the pebbles as it evaporates. Groups of plants can be arranged on a tray of moist pebbles.

Plant Food

Several good houseplant fertilizers are available at garden centers and other stores. Two that I am familiar with are Vigaro and Ra-Pid-Gro. These are soluble in water and should be given to most plants about every three weeks during the regular watering. Do not fertilize plants that are dormant or resting. Dormancy is part of the cycle of life of all plants. Some go about it more dramatically than others, losing their leaves and becoming generally bedraggled. Water should be gradually withheld from these plants and they should be removed to a dim area to rest. Give plant food when they start growing again. Other plants like Philodendron slow their growth and stop producing new shoots but they retain their attractive appearance. They can be left in place to continue their decorative function.

Light and Air

All plants need light to survive. Some need a lot of sun, others a reasonable amount, and still others need just good strong light. Some plants will tolerate dim areas but will grow more vigorously when they are exposed to better light. It is essential to know the light needs of the plants you are cultivating. All flowering plants, for instance, need sun. Foliage plants that grow in the shade in their native soil can tolerate less light than other plants. Houseplants need fresh air if they are to prosper. A frequently opened window on the opposite side of the room will usually be sufficient. Avoid exposing them to draughts and cold blasts of winter air.

Simple Plant Propogating

Houseplants have a varying life span. Some will inevitably grow old and shaggy and, sentiment to the contrary, should be replaced. If you know a few simple methods of plant propagation, you can replace the old plant with its own offspring. In addition, a knowledge of simple plant propagation will enable you to add to

Massed plants summering on terrace.

your collection of plants with slips and cuttings donated by generous friends.

The simplest way to propagate houseplants is to take a plant cutting and place it in water or a rooting medium until it roots. Take the cutting, containing four or five leaves, from a growing end of a plant, a place where the plant has recently put out new leaves or shoots. Snip it just below a point where a leaf joins the stem. Cuttings of many plants, Philodendron and Ivy, for instance, root easily in water. However, the rooted cutting sometimes cannot survive the transfer to a flowerpot. You can minimize the shock if, after the root system is established, you add a little soil to the water each day unil you have a fairly compact mass of mud.

At this point, you can transfer the plant to a pot, taking care not to disturb the roots.

If you prefer to root your cuttings in a rooting medium (and I do), dip the cutting end in a commercial rooting hormone like Rootone, then place it in a clay pot filled with moist vermiculite or perlite. Put the pot in a plastic bag and tie the bag shut. Keep the cutting, enclosed in the plastic bag, in dim light at a moderate temperature of about 68 degrees. Check after a week to see if growth has started. Just pull the stem gently from the rooting medium. If it resists at all, it has probably rooted. Don't be concerned if it hasn't, just give it more time.

Potting Houseplants

When your cuttings root, you'll have to pot them in regular soil. Choose two and a half inch clay pots with holes in the bottom. Place a small piece of broken flowerpot over the hole, curved side up, to permit drainage. Add good rich garden soil or a prepared mix, like African Violet soil, to the pot until it is almost half full. Spread the roots of the cutting very carefully and place them on top of the soil. Add more soil until it is within a half inch of the top of the pot. Press the soil down gently so that it is firmly packed. Water thoroughly, then place the seedling in a shaded spot until it is well established, about a week.

When a houseplant becomes pot-bound and its roots start growing out of the bottom of the pot, you'll have to decide whether you want it to remain the same size or grow larger. To prevent further growth, trim the exposed roots and replace some of the soil at the top of the pot with fresh soil. Some plants will require this growth-retarding treatment once or twice a year. If you wish the plant to increase in size, you will have to transfer it to a larger pot. Choose a pot that is just one size larger. An oversized pot can cause the plant's roots to rot. The repotting procedure for a mature plant is generally the same as for the rooted cuttings. Take care that the soil around the plant is dry so that you can remove the entire mass without disturbing the roots. Add soil to the larger pot until it is a third full, then place the plant with its roots encased in the old soil on top. Fill in with more soil and water thoroughly. Allow the plant to rest for a few days away from strong sunlight.

Easy to Grow Foliage Plants

If you are a novice or have never had success with houseplants, start all over now with Philodendrons. These undemanding plants have such a tenacious desire to survive that only the grossest neglect can subdue them. They are available in graceful vining varieties that are delightful for wall planters, handsome large-leaved, floor-standing specimens, and all variations in between. A little experience with Philodendrons will convince you either that you have grown a green thumb or that one isn't necessary. There are hundreds of varieties of Philodendrons growing wild in the jungles of Central or South America. There they have

Philodendron squamiferon   *Schefflera Actinophylla*

Aspidistra plant.

learned to withstand sudden downpours of rain and extended periods of drought. They climb up and around trees and have had to learn to flourish without sun. This ability to adjust to less than ideal circumstances has produced a superior houseplant.

Although only a comparatively few varieties of Philodendron are available as houseplants, these are ample for decorating needs. Unfortunately their names are in quite a muddle. Some plants like the *Monstera deliciosa,* misnamed *Philodendron pertusum,* are not Philodendrons at all, but their cultural needs are just about the same. The most common Philodendron is the small vining variety often available at the dime store. It is the heartleaf Philodendron, sometimes called *Philodendron cordatum* and just as frequently called *Philodendron oxycardium*. Cut-leaf Philodendron is the *Monstera deliciosa*. It has lovely large, cut leaves and will climb attractively up a moss-covered pole if one is provided. Another climber, the Fiddleleaf Philodendron, has large leaves somewhat reminiscent of a violin in shape. Other Philodendrons or near Philodendrons are just as decorative. *Philodendron squamiferum* has dagger-shaped leaves covered with tiny red hairs. *Philodendron dubium,* another cut-leaf Philodendron, has large lacy leaves. *Philodendron Wendlandi* with long narrow leaves and *Philodendron selloum* are among the easiest to grow. Unfortunately, since their botanical names are misused at the florist and garden center, as well as by some plant experts, it is sometimes difficult to get what you ask for. However, if a plant is called Philodendron, you can assume that it will be easy to care for. Some varieties prefer more light than others, but all grow fairly well wherever they are placed. The small heartleaf Philodendron and similar types sometimes become leggy especially if they do not get a lot of light. If this happens, cut off the straggling ends and propagate them in water or vermiculite as discussed previously. Culture for Philodendrons is the same as discussed in general culture. They do not like excessive sunlight.

The Aspidistra is another easygoing plant. A native of China, tough, almost indestructible, it has been around for a long time. It achieved its greatest popularity during the Victorian era, when it graced the overblown parlors and men-only saloons of the period with equal aplomb. In the saloons it survived a standard diet of cigar butts and beer and earned its nickname: "the cast-iron plant." It is really a handsome plant with long, graceful, dark-green leaves that can be clipped for flower arrangements. It is so long lived that a mature plant is a good investment. Although the Aspidistra will survive almost any circumstances, it will reward good care with a luxuriant appearance. Keep it out of direct sunlight but place it in a light area. Wash the leaves regularly and follow general cultural suggestions. This plant can be lifted and divided every few years if you wish. To propagate

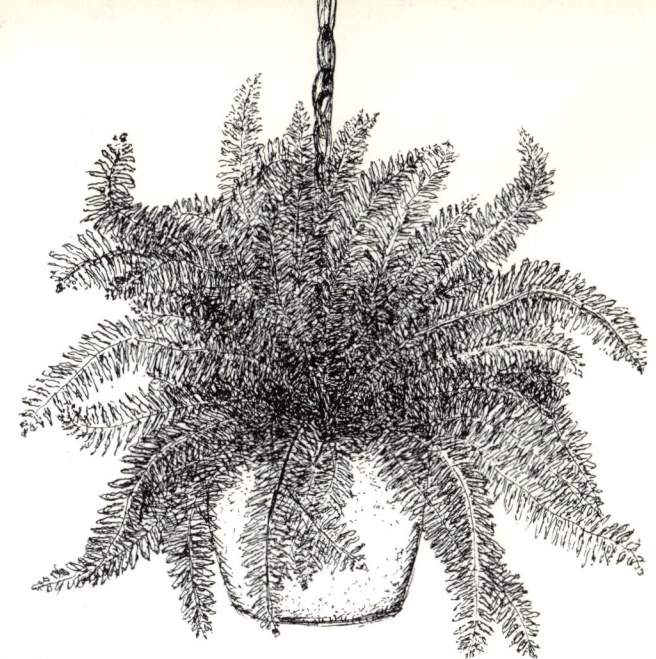

Boston Fern in hanging basket.

by this method, allow the soil to become somewhat dry, then remove the plant from the pot and separate the roots gently. Repot in two pots following the suggestions in the section on potting. Aspidistras are handsome accessories for large chests or tables or on their own in a plant stand.

The Boston Fern is another popular decorative plant. It is not quite as undemanding as the Aspidistra or Philodendron, but with reasonable care and respect for its needs it will prosper. The Boston Fern is a sport or mutation of a Sword Fern, *Nephrolepis exaltata,* that grows wild in parts of Florida, in South America, and in Africa and eastern Asia. A new attractive mutation with the same cultural needs is called Boston Curly. These Ferns grow best away from strong sunlight but they do need a bright area and a moist atmosphere. You can provide additional humidity with moist pebbles as described in the section on humidity. A large healthy Fern is very decorative in a hanging basket. Incidentally it won't like being moved about so decide carefully where it will look best and then leave it there. Follow general cultural suggestions and don't ever allow it to dry out. Wipe the leaves with a damp cloth at regular intervals.

Wandering Jew is the popular name for several very charming plants with the same cultural needs. These are the *Zebrina pendula, Tradescantia fluminensis,* and *Commelina nudiflora.* All are rapidly growing and are delightful in hanging baskets or gracefully curving out of a wall planter. They do best in indirect sunlight but are very tolerant of shade and can be placed almost anywhere. Their need for moisture makes them ideal decorative accents in the bath. If the plants become leggy, take cuttings from the growing tips and root them in water or vermiculite as suggested in the section on plant progagation. These plants incidentally will grow for extended periods in water alone. For pot culture, follow the suggestions in the section on general culture. Do not let the plant dry out between waterings.

Flowering Plants

Flowering plants need more attention than foliage plants if they are to produce blooms. One of the easiest and most rewarding flowering plants for indoor culture is the zonal Geranium, *Pelargonium hortorum.* It is available with red, pink, white, or lavender flowers. All have the characteristic brownish green zone at the base of their leaves. Geraniums are natives of South Africa. Like all flowering plants they need full sun several hours a day, and should be placed on a shelf or plant stand in a sunny window. Of course you can enjoy their vibrant color for a few hours or an evening in other parts of the room. The plants make an especially charming centerpiece massed together in the middle of the dining table.

Massed Geraniums for a centerpiece.

Geraniums will bloom best if they are kept in pots that seem too small for their size. Give them plant food only when they are in bloom, and then give it as often as every two weeks. Pretty plants require care. To produce a round full plant with a profusion of blooms, pinch back the terminal shoots regularly during the early growth of the plant. When budded stems appear, discontinue pinching. You can propagate Geraniums easily if you take a cutting about five inches long with several leaves. Root it in water if you wish, but best results can be obtained if you follow the suggestions for rooting cuttings in vermiculite in the section on plant propagation. If you garden, you can plant Geraniums in the spring and take cuttings in late September before frost danger. These will root quickly, and before long they'll be producing blooms. If you remove faded blooms promptly, you can prolong the blooming period.

Forcing Spring Flowering Bulbs

You can have a delightful sample of springtime in winter if you force spring flowering bulbs. The easiest bulbs to force are the Paper-White Narcissus because they do not need a period of cold storage. Buy top-quality bulbs in the fall of the year. You'll need a bowl several inches deep and some white stones or pebbles. Fill the bowl half full of pebbles and add water just to the top of the pebbles. Place the bulbs, pointed side up, on top of the pebbles about a half inch apart. The bottom of the bulb should be in the water. Add more pebbles, almost to the necks of the bulbs; then place the bowl of bulbs in a cool dark place, perhaps the basement. Sixty degrees is about as warm as they can stand, and a cooler temperature is preferable. Check the water level daily and keep the bottom of the bulbs constantly wet. After two or three weeks check for shoots and vigorous root growth. If it is well established, move the bowl to a sunny window. Keep the bulbs watered, and the lovely flowers should appear in a few weeks.

Other spring flowering bulbs, like Crocus, Daffodils, and Tulips, need a cold period before they can produce flowers. If you want to force these varieties, you can place them in the vegetable crisper of your refrigerator for two months, perhaps in October.

Place a thermometer in there with them because the temperature must be a pretty constant forty degrees. At the end of two months, plant the bulbs in bulb pots; these are lower and wider than regular flowerpots. Fill the pot half full of African Violet soil mix or rich garden soil. Place the bulbs a half inch apart, pointed side up on the soil, and then cover them up to their necks with the remaining soil. If the shoots are well out of the necks of the bulbs, place them immediately in a sunny window, otherwise put the pot in a dark cool place for a week or so. Water regularly in either case. Success with bulb forcing is always variable, but it's easy and fun to try. If you are successful, the beautifully delicate flowers in midwinter are a delight.

Plants for the Kitchen

A window garden of herbs is a perfect decorative accent for the kitchen. Their culture is simple and undemanding. The plants need sun, a fairly cool temperature, and some humidity, which you can provide with moist pebbles. If you have a window that receives a moderate amount of sunshine each day, this will be fine. If not, or if you have a kitchen without windows, which is popular in some apartments just now, you may want to grow the herbs on a shelf on the wall between the upper and lower cupboards. You'll have to install a fluorescent light above them and leave it on most of the day but the effect is charming—especially cheering in an inside room.

You can grow a single plant perhaps in a stoneware crock, anywhere that it will get some sun and good strong light. A vigorously growing Parsley plant is attractive centered on the

Parsley plant in stoneware crock.

breakfast table or bar. A window garden can be arranged with perhaps one or two plants growing in hanging baskets and the rest in a planter on the sill. You may be able to obtain herb plants from a local nursery, otherwise use the mail order sources listed at the end of this chapter. Spring or fall is the best time to start your plants. Once you become interested in herbs, you will soon have your own favorites. As a start, here are some herbs that will grow fairly easily indoors, with a few comments about their culture and background.

Chives
> This is a perennial herb. Snip pieces for culinary use from the sides to maintain a pleasingly shaped plant. Very long lasting.

Mint
> The variety *Mentha requieni,* a native of Corsica, is attractive in a hanging basket. Usually planted in the rock garden, it will creep invitingly over the edge of the basket. It has tiny extremely fragrant leaves. Perennial.

Parsley
> The Romans used this handsome herb to flavor broths. The early colonists brought it to this country. It is a biennial and should be discarded and replaced when it has seen its best days. Clip from the sides of the plant.

Rosemary
> The tradition of remembrance has been associated with Rosemary for centuries. At one time a bride carried a sprig in her bouquet to symbolize the happy memories of childhood that she would keep with her in her new home. The creeping variety of Rosemary, *Rosemary officinalis prostratus,* is another good plant for a hanging basket. Try adding a few chopped Rosemary leaves to the dumpling batter, for a stew. Marvelous. Rosemary is a perennial.

Sweet Woodruff
> A perennial herb used in Germany to make *Maiwein.* Clip from the sides of the plant to control growth. Perhaps I include this herb because I had my first glass of *Maiwein* under delightfully youthful circumstances. In springtime, I

like to steep a few sprigs in a bottle of Moselle wine an hour or two before serving chilled.

More Herbs for Indoor Culture:

Catnip	*Perennial, keep pruned or plant gets scraggly*
Lemon Verbena	*Perennial, difficult, needs good sun, use the leaves to flavor jelly, or for potpourri*
Sage	*Perennial, choose dwarf variety, cut from sides*
Sweet Basil	*Annual, choose a small variety*
Sweet Marjoram	*Perennial, gray foliage, clip from sides*
Thyme	*Perennial, clip from sides*

Scented-leaved Geraniums

Scented-leaved Geraniums are usually grown in the indoor herb garden because their cultural requirements are the same, but they will flourish in any sunny window. There are more than two hundred varieties with different scents and variations of scents, but only a relatively few are easily obtainable. Small in size and especially attractive in the window garden are those with scents of Orange, Lime, Ginger, and Apple. The Peppermint-scented variety, *Pelargonium tomentosum,* is a sprawling type that can be used to good advantage in a hanging basket. Rose Geranium, *Pelargonium graveolens,* is a full-sized plant with lavender flowers and the soft scent of Roses. It's fun to experiment with the different kinds and settle on a few favorites. Hybridizers are constantly crossing varieties and obtaining even more compelling combinations of scents. Use the leaves for potpourri or sachet mixtures or just enjoy their subtle fragrance in your home.

Do It Yourself Plants

In my grandmother's kitchen, a Sweet Potato vine used to curve up and around the frame of a double window. It was charming, and not the least of its charm came from the fact that it had grown from a lowly tuber. There is something intriguing about a gay climbing vine or handsome potted plant coming from a leftover. A good-sized foliage plant can be grown from an Avocado pit. Just remove the outer covering and soak the seed in warm water overnight. Then place the seed pointed side up in a pot of African Violet soil mix or good garden soil. It should be just beneath the surface. Keep moist but not waterlogged in a dim area. After three or four weeks, the plant should push through the soil. Move it to a sunny window and give plant food regularly, following the suggestions in the section on general culture.

The top of a Pineapple will grow into an unusual spiky plant and very occasionally it will produce a miniature Pineapple of its own. Just slice off the top of a Pineapple, taking about an inch of the fruit. Plant this about an inch deep in good soil, top up. Keep moist and when roots form, move it to a sunny window and follow general cultural suggestions. Like the Avocado, this plant needs full sun.

The Sweet Potato vine is very easy to grow but you must select a tuber with eyes. Put it in a tightly fitting full glass of water, half in and half out, then place the glass in a light but not sunny place. The vine should sprout very quickly, and then should be moved to a sunny window. You can leave it in the water or plant it in a pot of good soil. Since the vine likes the sun and the root doesn't, potting seems the best solution. Follow general cultural suggestions.

Special Plantings and Decorative Ideas

Miniatures

There are a good many attractive miniature plants but quite a few need special attention and are not too practical for decorative use. The most easygoing and readily available miniatures are the Cacti. These tiny plants are frequently immature forms of larger plants that grow slowly enough to retain their miniature status almost indefinitely. Their most important cultural requirement is full sun. They should be allowed to dry out completely between waterings and it is not necessary to provide humidity. Miniature Cacti are available in a variety of fascinating forms, one and two inches high, often at the dime store.

Cacti mixed.

On a shelf in a window or perhaps on a small writing desk beside a sunny window, you can set up a small display stand, using children's square blocks. Paint the blocks a shiny black and arrange them in levels of one, two, and three blocks, close together. Then place the different forms of Cacti on these small stands. Floral clay or glue will hold the blocks together.

Cacti in small dish garden.

You can make a charming dish garden quite easily, with seven or eight little plants. A low ceramic dish filled with white or black polished stones would be attractive. Just leave the Cactus plants in their pots and sink them in the stones so that the pots are hidden and the plants seem to be growing out of the stones. Arrange the plants to highlight their contrast of forms and textures. This tiny garden would be pleasing on a side table near a window where it will receive the sun it needs.

Terrariums

A terrarium filled with small foliage or flowering plants is a delightful conversation piece. Actually a miniature greenhouse, it is a direct descendant of the Wardian case, a popular parlor decoration in Victorian times. The small glass case was invented or discovered by Nathaniel B. Ward. In the course of an experiment in 1829, Mr. Ward placed a dead insect in mold and put it into a closed glass jar. After a while some vegetation appeared on the mold and the idea for the Wardian case evolved.

African Violets in terrarium.

Terrariums are easy to construct. You can use a large brandy snifter or even a discarded fish bowl for a container, with a flat piece of glass or plastic for a cover. To prepare the terrarium for plants, you'll need some planter moss, stones or gravel, and good garden soil or African Violet soil mix. Line the sides and bottom of the container below the soil level with the moss placed with the green side against the glass. Next put a one-inch layer of gravel or stones in the bottom of the container. Add about two inches of soil. Place a selection of small plants carefully in the soil and spray the soil lightly with water. Cover the terrarium and place it where it will have good light but absolutely no sun. Water sparingly only when necessary, which won't be often. If the inside of the terrarium becomes foggy, open the cover slightly.

Plants that like high humidity do very well in a terrarium. African Violets planted by themselves are strikingly decorative for a coffee table. Take care not to touch their leaves or let water fall on them. Many other plants are suitable, and small gardens can be planted using a variety of vines and tiny upright plants with perhaps a few stones. A list of decorative plants at the end of the chapter indicates some that are suitable for terrarium culture.

Hanging Baskets

Hanging arrangements of plants are like living mobiles. Light and shimmering, suspended in space, their decorative effect is lovely. Hanging containers to hold the plants are available in a variety of shapes and sizes and materials. Some are no more than wire frames which are lined with sheet moss and filled with garden soil. These have the disadvantage of needing water every day and of dripping over everything when they get it. Best to use them on the patio if at all. New self-watering pots are available which perform their decorative function with very little care and are handsome holding a large fern or other luxuriant plant. Mail order sources for these containers are noted at the end of the chapter. To pot plants in these containers follow the same procedure suggested in the section on potting. Another good container for indoor or patio plants is a hanging ceramic container in which the plant is left in its clay pot and placed on a layer of moist pebbles for added humidity. Plants in these containers are easy to care for, don't drip, and are very decorative. Hanging baskets which will hold potted plants are also attractive, but the plant must be removed frequently for watering. It is usually impossible to add moist pebbles, but some baskets are so interesting that these faults can perhaps be overlooked. Hanging plants can be enjoyed almost anywhere. High over the sink in the kitchen; perhaps two at different levels in a dining-room window; or one or two over a low chest in a hall. For the tiny bathroom they are invaluable, adding a bright accent where space is limited. Plants suitable for hanging containers are noted in the following list of decorative plants.

Hanging plants.

A Victorian wire plant stand holding flowering and foliage plants adds a garden effect to one end of a formal bedroom!

Delightful idea for an informal area: a built-in planter. The plants are left in their clay pots and placed on the moist pebbles.

List of Decorative Plants for the Home

	Trailing or Vining	Needs Sun	Strong Light	Tolerates Dim Light	Terrarium	Hanging
African Violets (*Saintpaulia*)			•		•	
Boston Fern (*Nephrolepis exaltata*)			•			•
Croton		•	•		•	
Dieffenbachia			•	•		
Asparagus sprengeri	•		•	•		•
Jade Plant (*Crassula*)		•	•			
Spider Plant	•		•	•		•
Rubber Plant			•			
Aspidistra			•	•		
Philodendron	•		•	•	•	•
Norfolk Island Pine			•			
Peperomia			•	•		
Sansevieria			•			
Wandering Jew (all varieties)	•		•	•	•	•
Ivy (*Hedera helix*)	•	•	•		•	•

All these plants are fairly easy to care for. Their light needs have been noted in a general way and their decorative use.

Mail Order Sources:

Geo. W. Park Seed Co., Inc.
Greenwood, S.C. 29646

Some houseplants. Several attractive and practical hanging containers including self-watering. Catalogue.

Merry Gardens
Camden, Me. 04843

Houseplants and herbs. Catalogue.

House Plant Corner
Oxford, Md. 21654

Excellent selection of houseplants and equipment. Catalogue.

Cook's Geranium Nursery
Lyons, Kans. 67554

Geraniums, including scented-leaved.

Tinari Greenhouses
2325 Valley Rd.
Huntingdon Valley, Penna. 19006

African violets.

Chapter Six

Fruits and Vegetables

A farmers' market is the place to see fresh fruits and vegetables in all their remarkable profusion of color and texture and form. A farm may show us some fruits and some vegetables in their natural growing state, but the selection of crops is necessarily limited. At a large market, one can begin to grasp the infinite variety of this bounty of the natural world. Most cities of any size have some form of market for wholesale if not retail sales. Visit one if you can, early in the morning when the day is just slipping into place. The vigorous sound of trucks backing, gears shifting, boxes being bumped and scraped, and shouts of warning and greeting offer striking contrast to the delicacy of the produce being unloaded. Look at the forms of the fruits and vegetables as if you were seeing them for the first time. Think of their excitingly sculptured shapes instead of their culinary potential. Rub the shaggy round brown Coconut ball and brush the smooth ivory Mushroom buttons. Look at the warty mottled crooks of yellow Squash and see the overblown, purple streaked, red Cabbage rosettes, the perfect teardrop contour of a pale yellow Pear.

Before very long, just looking at these interesting natural forms will stimulate decorative ideas.

If you can't get to a market, a vegetable store managed by someone with feeling for his wares is a fairly good substitute. In New York some years ago, we used to know an Italian greengrocer whose shop was a pleasure to see. Pineapples with their thrust of swordlike leaves were placed one above the other, leading the eye to a mound of red satin Tomatoes. Yellow Bananas with streaks of green were tucked in radiating hands above the grayish mesh of Muskmelons. Glistening Eggplants, purple misted Plums, dark green acorn Squash with just a brush of bright orange provided color and textural contrasts that delighted the eye. Market displays are stimulating and they can inspire arrangements of fruits and vegetables that are especially appropriate for patio or porch dinners.

If you want to try one, use a little box about ten inches square overturned to provide for the cascading effect in the market.

Basket of decorative possibilities.

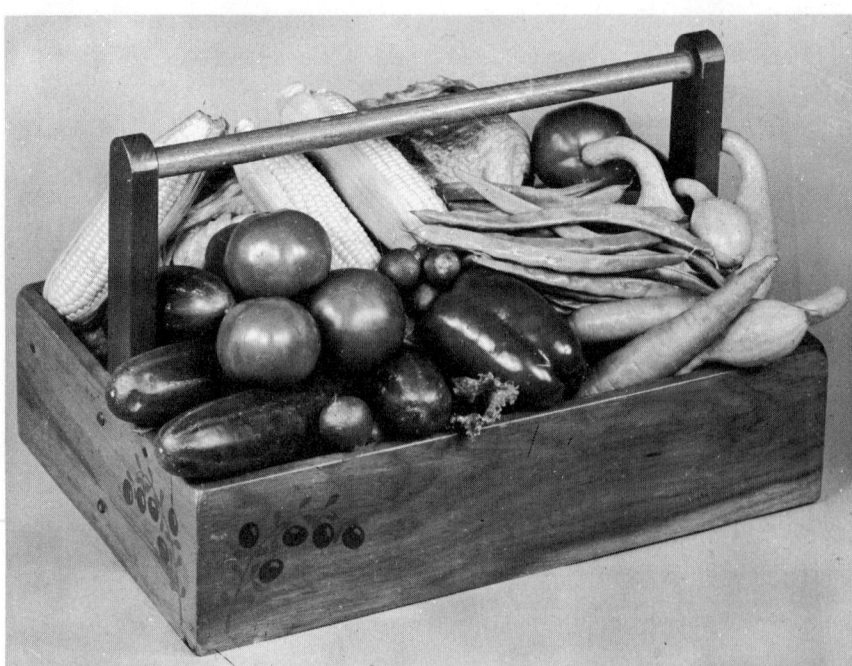

A tall floor-standing plant fills one corner of this dining room with soft green patterns, relieving the severity of the decor. The large bouquet adds a necessary splash of vivid color, a good foil for the pale background. The red apple in the fruit basket subtly repeats the color accent.

The large airy yellow and white bouquet of flowers centered on the dining table repeats the graceful curves of the chandelier and adds bright color that complements the darker walls and drapery in this room. The green fern beside the blue and gold drapery is a subtly conceived color accent.

The appeal of the wood surfaces in this rustic entry is heightened by the plant materials. The pale beige of the dried plant stalks in the floor-standing bouquet offers an interesting color contrast to the dark paneled door. The deep green of the foliage of the floor-standing plant on one side and the hanging plant on the other help to co-ordinate the dark wood of the door with the light wood walls. The touch of orange provided by the small dried bouquet on the shelf provides a unifying accent.

Dried plant materials in colors that range from pale beige through brown and very soft orange are arranged simply in an interesting hanging container. Their colors blend beautifully with the wood-paneled walls and harmonize with the pillows on the sofas as well as with the straw of the handmade broom. This interplay of muted color provides a foil for the vivid blues and greens in the room.

The color scheme of this cheerful breakfast room is complemented by the colors of the foliage and flowers in the enclosed garden outside the window, a charming idea for any window with a poor view. The large bouquet centered on the table repeats the orange centers of the flowers in the wallpaper and cloth. The green napkins and the chair seats link the green in the wallpaper with the foliage in the outside garden.

The natural colors of the fruit in the bowl on the table accent the sofa and chair colors as well as the colors in the painting over the fireplace in this charming room. Notice the co-ordinated bouquets of daisies and foliage on either side of the fireplace. The white flowers and containers complement the ornamental jars on the mantle and the large table lamp. Fern plants inside the fireplace pick up the green in the chair covers.

This charming corner is made more so by the lavish use of natural materials. The overflowing bouquet of orange flowers blends well with the colors of the tea wagon and bench and the darker wood of the corner cupboard. The bowl of fruit repeats both container and flower colors, and next to it a little bouquet of daisies complements the window treatment and calls attention to the milk glass collection on the shelf in the cupboard above. On top of the cupboard, a white container holds green foliage that provides a necessary strong dark color accent.

The oversized bouquet of flowering Dogwood expresses the airy gaiety of this delightful room, while the white flowers emphasize the white accents. The Philodendron plant placed next to a white lamp picks up the green and white of the bouquet and increases its decorative impact. The bowl of fruit, apples, and strawberries repeats the dominant room color against the white table.

The soft green of the foliage plants against the wall of this charming study emphasizes the creamy color scheme which is complemented by a small basket of flowers on the desk. The green ribbon on the basket handle subtly calls attention to the color statement of the foliage. Notice that the natural tones of the feathers color-blend with the design on the shades and with the small basket.

A large basket of garden flowers brings needed color to one corner of this interesting room. Notice the small bouquet on the cabinet on the other side of the fireplace that is color matched to this large one. Both bouquets complement the throw pillow on the dark chair and the red upholstery of the facing chair. An interesting color accent is provided by the bowl of oranges matched to the small orange box on the table. The deep green color of the foliage plant on the hearth balances the strong solid blocks of color in the chairs.

Fruit market arrangement.

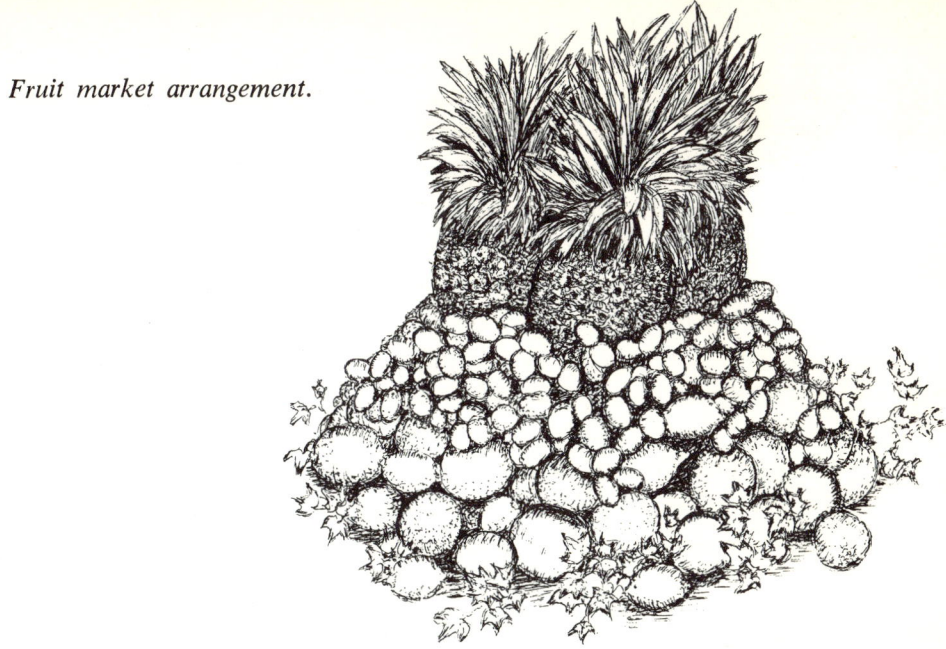

A fruit arrangement placed at one end of the table against a wall is attractive. Use your choice of fruits or try this arrangement, which needs three Pineapples, four or five bunches of Grapes, and two dozen Oranges, Lemons, and Limes mixed. Condition the fruit as described later in this chapter, then flatten a good-sized piece of floral clay on top of the little box. On the clay, place the three Pineapples, upright and close together. Now pile the citrus fruit around the bottom of the box, using small pieces of floral clay, if necessary, to hold them together. From the top of the box, cascade bunches of Grapes all around. To hold them in place, use old-fashioned hairpins hooked around the top of the grape stems and pushed at a slight downward angle into the bottoms of the Pineapples or the clay. Complete the arrangement with sprigs of small leaves tucked in around the Pineapples, between the bunches of Grapes, and around the bottom of the fruit.

The variety of fruits and vegetables brought into our local markets is staggering. Their native lands encompass the world. Most in some form have nourished mankind for thousands of years. Lettuce in its hundreds of crisp, curly, smooth, and leafy variations is a descendant of a wayside weed that grew centuries ago in Asia Minor, one that is distantly related to our wild

Hawkweed. Some type of Lettuce has been cultivated for at least two thousand years. Incidentally a salad, spelled salat, of the past was apt to be more daring than ours. In the Middle Ages, it might have been made from many kinds of herbs and flowers and frequently included those enemies of the suburban lawn, Dandelion and Chickweed, all dressed with salt. Broccoli with its velvet-like heads of blue-green buds is a comparative newcomer to our country, although it was a popular vegetable in Greece and Italy for centuries. Immigrants from those two countries brought seeds with them and cultivated the handsome vegetable in garden plots beside their new homes, especially in the suburbs of Boston and on Staten Island in New York. Broccoli has been commercially grown here only since the beginning of this century, most of it in California. Broccoli and Cauliflower are closely related and both are considered botanically to be variations of Cabbage, which is a truly ancient vegetable. The wild ancestor of the Cabbage has never been positively identified, perhaps because it has been cultivated for at least four thousand years. This robust vegetable was grown in early American gardens at the end of the seventeenth century and probably before.

Fruits have an equally long history. The ancient Egyptians produced Grapes for wine in carefully cultivated vineyards. Pomegranates and Figs as well as Grapes were Egyptian symbols of fertility.

Most citrus fruits are natives of Asia, but they were already familiar delights in the ancient days of Rome and Greece and Egypt. Fruits in variety, often combined with flowers, added color to the sumptuous banquets of all three countries. The Romans favored garlands of fruits and vegetables arranged with foliage and pine cones and nuts, an idea that can be borrowed today for long low arrangements attractively placed down the center of the dining table. The talented Della Robbia family of fifteenth-century Italy used these same forms in the terra cotta sculptures that inspire many of our most attractive Christmas wreaths.

Awareness of the beauty inherent in the forms of fruits and vegetables is apparent in the stone carving and tapestries and illuminated manuscripts of the Middle Ages. The examples that survive show concentrated attention to detail and decorative

A cone of fresh fruits centered in a circle of fruit—in the eighteenth-century manner at Colonial Williamsburg.

effect. Closer to our own day on a magnificent scale, the stone columns of the Capitol Building in Washington, D.C., are crowned with beautifully executed stone-carved forms of Corn and Tobacco to symbolize the importance of these two plants in the lives of the early colonists.

For centuries, fruits and vegetables had been arranged with skill and imagination at banquets and fetes. The eighteenth-century custom of centering the banquet table with an ornate epergne to hold fruits and sweetmeats may well have evolved from these earlier traditions. When the Pineapple was introduced into England from Central America, its exotic form caught the fancy of the fashionable. It was a popular crown for the epergne and inspired the beautifully carved Pineapple finials that embellished fine furniture of the period. This fruit's curious English name came directly from its appearance, which reminded some people of a pine cone. It had been called Ananas in Central America, and indeed that name still holds in France and Germany today.

As might be expected, the Asian approach toward the arrangement of fruits and vegetables is lighter and more delicate than the European. More emphasis is placed on the beauty of a single fruit than on the generous display of many. Contemporary Japanese might place two or three perfect pieces of fruit on several pressed Fern leaves, for instance, an idea that might be borrowed for a luncheon centerpiece or used to add interest to a small sideboard. Often fruit is left on a sparsely leaved branch and

Fruits in a low basket tray add color to this informal dining area.

displayed quite simply and naturally. An arrangement using this idea would be very attractive in a wall-hung vase, perhaps in a breakfast room. If you decide to try it, you will need four branches, one with two pieces of fruit still attached. Do not condition the branches but prune them extensively to remove most of the leaves and any distracting cross branches and stems. Have your wall vase in place with water and a small piece of crumpled wire inside. The longest branch with two pieces of fruit still attached will look best if it is about twice the length of the vase. Place it curving out one side of the vase. Place a shorter branch curving upward against the wall and arrange the two shortest branches so that they curve out and over the rim of the vase.

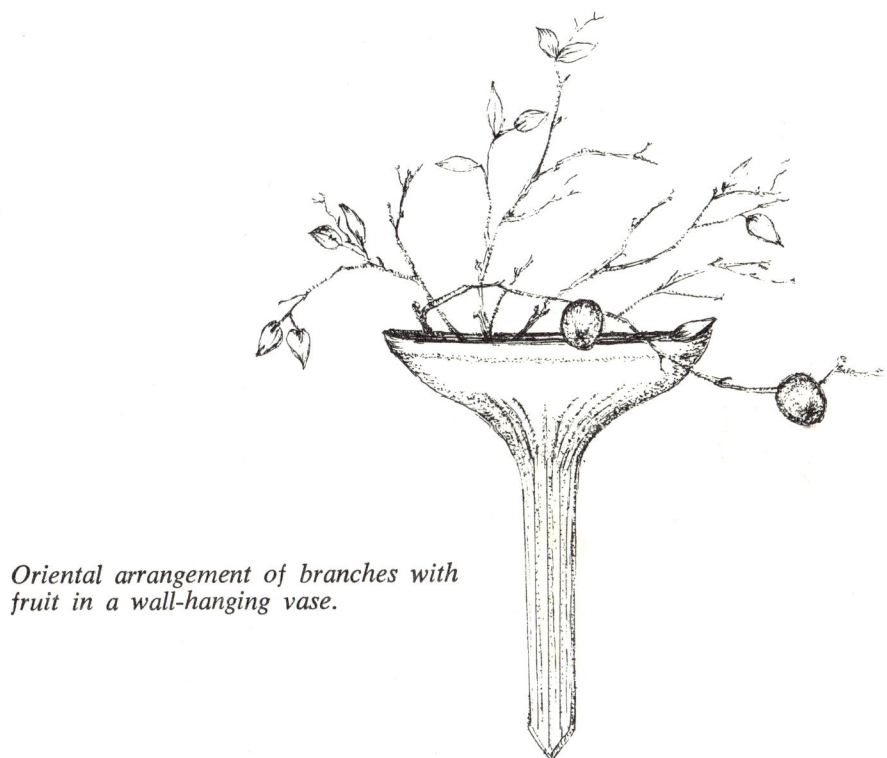

Oriental arrangement of branches with fruit in a wall-hanging vase.

Sources of Fruits and Vegetables

Although you might want to raise your own ornamental Corn and Gourds and perhaps a few Artichokes for drying, the vegetable market is the most dependable source of supply for a variety of fruits and vegetables for decorating. Choose one that has a good selection of absolutely fresh produce attractively displayed. The keeping qualities of fruits and vegetables used in arrangements can be a problem. A list at the end of this chapter gives an indication of how long you can expect them to retain their attractive appearance.

Selecting and Conditioning

To extend the decorative life of fruits and vegetables, choose those that feel a little heavy for their size. They should be somewhat underripe but not so much so that the color is impaired. At home, store them immediately in the crisper section of your refrigerator, then just before arranging, submerge your choice in ice water for about an hour. This treatment will extend their decorative life and eliminate many characteristic odors. Members of the Cabbage family especially need this aid. Cranberries are the only exception to this suggestion. Soaking in water hastens their demise.

Decorating with Fresh Fruits and Vegetables

A bowl of fruit crowned with a graceful cascade of Grapes is always attractive, but don't be limited by this convention. When you are in the market, try to see the decorative potential in a few stalks of Broccoli, for instance, or an Artichoke, or a few bulbs of Garlic. A little imagination can provide your home with unique decorative accents.

Perhaps because fruits and vegetables are primarily foods, we are reluctant to use them frivolously. It is true that most of them, if displayed as long as a flower arrangement, will not be fit to eat. If this waste seems unconscionable, stick to the varieties that will not be damaged by extended display (see list at the end of the chapter). In addition, place fruits in small decorative containers about the house for eating as well as decoration. A white, footed container filled with a few perfect red Apples would be a striking accent on a side table.

Fruits are admirably suited to the dining room. A basket of Mint arranged with Plums or Strawberries is a delightful eye opener for the breakfast table. It's simple to do—just line a

Footed container of Apples with Ivy.

small basket with plastic and then foil. Cut a piece of Oasis to fit the basket, soak it in water, and place it in the basket. With a pencil, make small holes fairly close together in the Oasis. Fill the holes with sprigs of Mint (or Rosemary or even Parsley). Then arrange the fruit in the green foliage. The foliage will last a long time if you remember to add additional water as needed. The fruit can be eaten and replaced perhaps every other day with little effort. A scattering of flowers in fruit arrangements is a delightful accent. You can keep the flowers fresh in small water-filled water picks that can be hidden beneath the fruit. The water picks are available at many florists and by mail order.

Ready for Halloween: plump Coconuts, red Apples, and nuts piled casually around the candles make an unusual autumn centerpiece.

Pyramids of Lemons and Limes arranged on shining foliage with the green and yellow fruits alternating make an attractive centerpiece. Placed on a pewter tray or a mat, the arrangement can be enjoyed on a side table or chest as well.

A brown stoneware bowl filled with Oranges and Kumquats and a few sprigs of green foliage would be an attractive and fairly lasting accessory for a family room or other informal area.

The decorative possibilities of many vegetables are frequently overlooked. Of course in the fall of the year, Squash or Pumpkins are often seen arranged with autumn leaves on a buffet or chest, but the wide variety of vegetables at our disposal can provide many more interesting combinations. Even the most perishable vegetable can be enjoyed in a centerpiece for one meal and then removed with the crumbs, perhaps to turn up the next day in a delicious casserole. Bright red Peppers contrasted against the dark green of Parsley are dramatic in a footed glass container. Broccoli can be cut short and impaled on a needlepoint holder in a low container like a green blossom with perhaps some Fern foliage added. Mushrooms are an intriguing centerpiece when arranged on a bed of Pine. A bowl of Tomatoes with small white flowers and single leaves of any available foliage makes a striking arrangement. For a luncheon you might try a basket of Asparagus spears arranged stiffly upright with flowers of the same height and strap leaves curving gracefully out to the sides. Of course, you'll develop exciting ideas of your own that will be just right for your home.

Fruits or vegetables that you want to use decoratively for an extended period should be preserved with varnish or a clear plastic spray. Vegetables and fruits treated in this way cannot be eaten later, of course. The treated fruits such as Lady Apples can be added to Christmas wreaths for a Della Robbia effect. Directions for making wreaths are in Chapter Eight. In addition, many attractive arrangements based on the Della Robbia style can be enjoyed during the Christmas season as well as at other times during the fall and winter. An arrangement circling a hurricane lamp is very effective on a chest, perhaps in an entry or in an upstairs hall. It's very easy to do, just surround the lamp with Evergreens or glycerinized leaves and pile the fruit casually on the

Asparagus spears arranged with flowers and strap leaves.

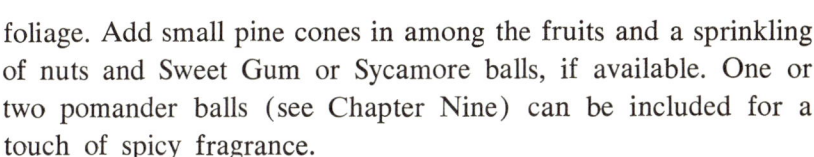

Broccoli with foliage.

foliage. Add small pine cones in among the fruits and a sprinkling of nuts and Sweet Gum or Sycamore balls, if available. One or two pomander balls (see Chapter Nine) can be included for a touch of spicy fragrance.

Drying Fruits and Vegetables

Dried materials because they are permanent are versatile decorating accessories. Unfortunately, few vegetables and even fewer fruits can be dried successfully. Those that can have been noted for quick reference in the list at the end of this chapter. Drying directions are given below. Some dried vegetables such as Gourds and Corn are available at the market in season. Dried Garlic bulbs can be found all year round of course. Fresh Artichokes, sweet Peppers and red Onions and Pomegranates are available fresh and can be dried successfully.

Pomegranates usually take several months to dry. Place them on a rack with a circulation of air above and below. The rack can be elevated if you support it on either side with bricks or blocks of wood. Put the drying Pomegranates in a dark dry place. An attic, again, is perfect, but if you are drying just a few, the back of a kitchen cupboard will do nicely. Check the fruit after two months—it should feel firm and dry. If it doesn't, let it dry for a few weeks longer. Some shrinking and color loss should be expected. Incidentally, this odd-shaped fruit is most ancient. The tree has been cultivated in southern Asia and some Mediterranean countries for thousands of years, and the fruit, whose seeds symbolized fertility, was frequently mentioned in the mythology of the ancient Greeks. Perhaps best known is the legend of Persephone, in which Persephone couldn't resist eating a few Pomegranate seeds when she visited the underworld. For each seed she ate, she had to return each year to spend a month in the underworld. During her stay, the earth grew barren and that was the beginning of winter.

Artichokes should be very fresh and unblemished if they are to dry attractively. Hang them in a dark dry area where there is some circulation of air. To do this, twist floral wire around the stem of the Artichoke and hang it with its head down. Dry several. You might want to give some an open rosette form. To do this, check the vegetable after about a week. The leaves should have become soft and pliable. Push small pieces of paper toweling down in between the leaves to force them open and then rehang. Check again after several weeks or a month. The vegetable should look and feel dry. If it is, remove the paper toweling from between the leaves and store or hang the artichoke until you are ready to use it in an arrangement.

Hot Peppers, the long thin kind, available in lovely chartreuse and yellow and red shades, are very decorative strung and hung to dry in the kitchen. The easiest way to do this is to thread a long piece of heavy floral wire through the Peppers, near the top of the vegetable. You can then twist the two ends of the wire together to form a circle of Peppers and hang this from a fixture in the kitchen. Disguise the top of the wire with a sprig of dried Rosemary or other dried foliage. Two circles entwined are colorful hung on the side of a kitchen cupboard. You can also leave the wire straight and attach the small Peppers at right angles down its length. If you do this, make a few twists at the bottom to prevent the Peppers from sliding off, then cover the twist with a sprig of dried herb foliage.

Red Onions can be hung to dry as well. These are very in-

Peppers strung in entwined wire circles.

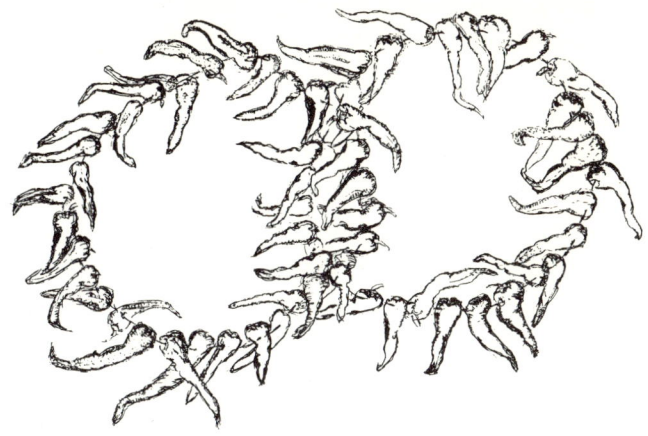

teresting strung with dried Garlic. A strong rope is needed and some thin floral wire. Make a loop in the top of the rope for hanging and lay it flat on a table. The Onions or Garlic will usually need just a twist of wire around their necks which can then be used to attach them to the rope. If the necks of the Onions or Garlic are short or the wire won't hold, you can take a large carpet needle, thread it with the thin wire, and draw this through the necks of the vegetables just above the base. In any case, to attach them to the rope, start at the bottom and wire them to the rope in groups of threes, working upward, so that the tiers will overlap when hung.

Gourds grown in your own garden should be picked for drying after the first frost. Wash them and dip them in a solution of household disinfectant like Lysol, then rinse and dry. With a hand or electric drill, make a tiny hole in the bottom of the Gourd and another at the top, beside the stem. They can be dried on a rack if you wish, but I have had complete success drying them in arrangements. Just be sure that there is a circulation of air around the arrangement. If you see any signs of decay remove the affected Gourd from the arrangement and redrill the holes, then place it on a rack to finish drying. After several months, shake the Gourds. If they are dry, the seeds will rattle. Spray them then with varnish or a clear plastic. Gourds that you purchase already dried at the market or elsewhere should have holes drilled in them as well. They are usually not completely dry and may rot without this precaution. Gourds dry so easily that one would think their marvelously varied cousins the Squashes would too. They won't. At least I have yet to find one that will. The only result of my experiments has been a wasted vegetable that might have been enjoyed in a tasty casserole.

Gourds can be strung together after they have been dried and hung where their unusual shapes and soft colors will contribute to your decorating scheme. Drill a hole all the way through the top of the vegetable about a half inch below the stem. If you think of it, this is best done before the Gourds are dry. Insert floral wire through the hole when the vegetable is dry and then spray it with varnish or clear plastic. Attach the Gourds to the rope as described for red Onions. Wire stemmed Strawflowers can be strung with the Gourds for an attractive effect. Several ropes are interesting hung in a corner of the kitchen or beside a fireplace in an informal room. These are charming patio decorations as well.

Ornamental Corn that you have grown yourself will dry easily. Pull the husks back into attractive curves and folds, then twist wire around the Corn where the husk meets the cob and tie

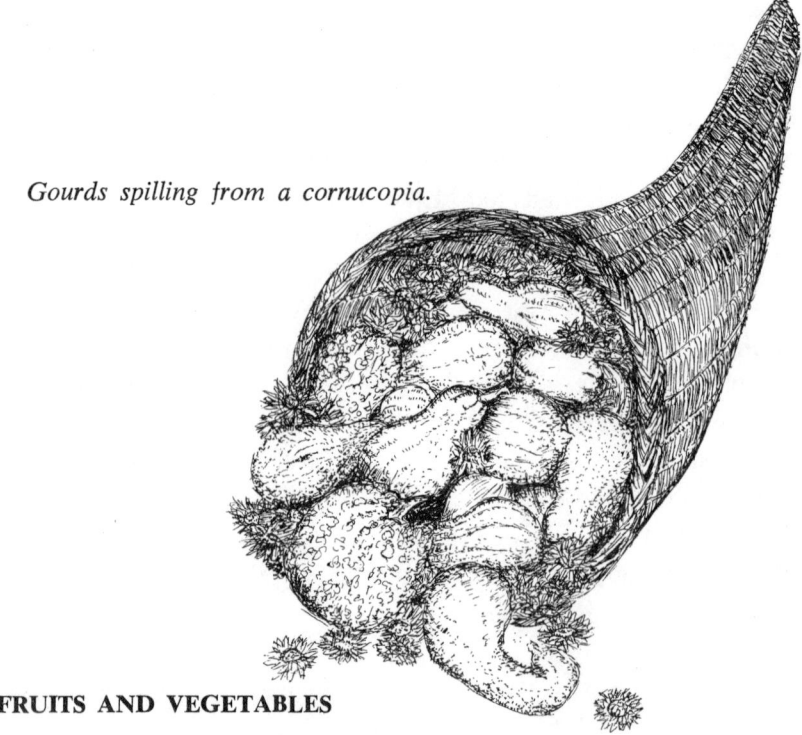

Gourds spilling from a cornucopia.

it to a line in a dark dry place. The Corn will be hanging at an angle. Remove it when the husks are crisp and dry and the kernels are hard. Store in tissue paper in a dry place or use immediately.

Decorative Ideas for Dried Vegetables

Dried vegetables are especially appropriate in the fall of the year. Eye-catching arrangements can be made with colorful autumn leaves, either dried or fresh (see Chapter Four), and two or three ears of Corn with a selection of Gourds. Very nice for a buffet or on a chest. A colorful display of Gourds with glycerinized Pittosporum or Ivy in a wall-hung basket can add color and charm to a small den or bedroom.

For a coffee table or perhaps on a divider, arrange dried Pomegranates in the curve of a piece of driftwood, then add a sweep of dried Broom in the background.

Gourds spilling from a cornucopia along with Strawflowers and Starflowers are a delightful accessory for a counter top or a shelf.

On the dining table center a handsome wooden tray or a wood burl and fill it with dried Artichokes and several bulbs of dried Garlic. These have no odor, by the way, and the effect is strikingly different.

Pomegranates and pomander balls (see Chapter Nine) accented with sprigs of dried Rosemary would be attractive in a footed container, placed perhaps in the living room where the fragrance would add subtly to the atmosphere. Combinations of dried vegetables are endless and lovely.

Miniatures

Miniature arrangements of fruits and vegetables are whimsical and fun to make. The idea is to find material in scale that resembles the full-sized variety. Containers can range from tiny mats of straw or coarse-weave linen to beautiful miniature reproductions of full-sized containers. Tiny baskets measuring two or three inches across are available at many variety stores. A full-sized arrangement of Cabbage and Broccoli and Cauliflower accented with sprigs of foliage and a sprinkling of Cranberries can be impersonated quite easily. A Brussels Sprout placed in the center of the arrangement becomes the Cabbage. Small florets of Cauliflower and Broccoli, pulled from the sides of the vegetables, will stand in for the full-sized variety. Privet or other small shrubbery berries can double for Cranberries, and small sprigs of herb foliage for the larger leaved varieties of foliage. A basket of Oranges and Apples can be simulated with single Kumquats and the miniature Apples produced by some forms of flowering ornamental Crabapple trees. Tuck in Mint leaves and diminutive Starflowers for a charming effect.

A Selection of Vegetables for Decorating

VEGETABLE	AVAILABLE	PEAK	KEEPING ABILITY DAYS	DRY
Artichoke	All year	Early spring	5	Yes
Asparagus	Feb.–June		3	
Beets	All year	June–Aug.	7–10	
Broccoli	All year	Oct.–Nov.	3	
Brussels Sprouts	Aug.–Mar.	Nov.	2	
Cabbage in variety	All year		4	
Carrots	All year		7–10	
Cauliflower	All year	Sept.–Nov.	2–3	
Corn	May–Nov.	June–Aug.	2–3	Yes
Cucumber	All year	May–Aug.	7	
Eggplant	All year		4–5	
Gourds	Oct.–Nov.		Indef.	Yes
Kohlrabi	May–Nov.	June–July	7–10	
Leeks	All year	June–Mar.	2–3	
Lettuce in variety	All year	May–Aug.	1	
Mushrooms	All year	Oct.–Feb.	4	
Onions	All year		20–30	Yes
Peppers	All year	June–Nov.	2–3	Hot Peppers can be dried

			KEEPING ABILITY	
VEGETABLE	AVAILABLE	PEAK	DAYS	DRY
Pumpkin	Oct.–Dec.		30	
Radish	All year	May–July	4–5	
Rutabagas	Aug.–Apr.		20–30	
Squash:				
Summer	All year	May–July	5	
Winter	Aug.–Feb.		20–30	
Tomatoes	All year	May–Aug.	3–4	
Turnips	All year	Oct.–Mar.	7–10	

			KEEPING ABILITY	
FRUITS	AVAILABLE	PEAK	DAYS	DRY
Apples in variety	Aug.–May		7–10	
Apricots	June–Aug.		2–3	
Avocado	All year	Dec.–Apr.	3–4	
Bananas	All year	Mar.–June	4	
Cranberries	Oct.–Jan.		7–10	
Grapefruit	All year	Oct.–May	3–4	
Grapes in variety	All year	Oct.–May	3–4	
Kumquats	Nov.–Feb.		10–14	
Lemon	All year	June–July	14	
Lime	June–Dec.		14	
Mango	May–Dec.		3–4	
Melons in variety	May Nov.		7	
Orange	Year round	Oct.–Mar.	5–7	
Peach	May–Oct.		3–4	
Pears in variety	Aug.–May		5	
Persimmon	Oct.–Feb.		2	
Pineapple	All year	Mar.–June	3–4	
Plum	June–Oct.		3–4	
Pomegranate	Sept.–Nov.		2–3	Yes
Tangerine	Dec.–Apr.		7	

Chapter Seven

Driftwood

There was a time when driftwood was just wood that had washed ashore on some windswept beach and lain there while the elements changed it into a piece of natural sculpture. It might be admired for its eroded lines and silvery patina, but not until recently has driftwood been widely appreciated in home decorating.

In primitive societies, wood was an important material from which to produce necessary bowls and utensils, or from which to carve religiously symbolic objects. The American Indian created complex totem poles from wood. Early African people made elongated figures and masks. Tradition holds that the first Christian cross was crudely hewn from natural wood. These early skills were gradually refined, and wood carving evolved into a thoughtfully executed art. The wooden choir stalls and altarpieces of European cathedrals of the twelfth to fifteenth centuries show examples of exquisite embellishment. Later, cabinetmakers and architects added decoratively carved forms to the homes they designed and the furniture they produced. In some of the lovely homes of the eighteenth and early nineteenth centuries, still standing, one can see beautifully detailed coping as well as delicately carved posts and finials. The refinement of wood, the beauty of finish and embellishment was more appreciated than the wood in its natural state. In a vast underpopulated world, this might be expected, or perhaps it is our Western heritage to appreciate the transformation of nature by man, rather than the natural object.

In the colonization of our country, each settler, of necessity, became intimately aware of the qualities of the trees around him. They were a source of utensils and equipment as well as a hobby for his limited leisure time. He learned the best trees for splits, which he could quarter and divide down the grain to have strips for the baskets which are admired so much today for the clean simplicity of their design. He made baskets for eggs, and for seed carrying, and baskets shaped to fit the shoulders of a mule. He knew which wood made the best shuttle for the loom his wife used to weave cloth for the family's clothing. He knew the best woods for making chairs and wagon wheels and tables and bedsteads. The same craftsman kept a small piece of wood with him to whittle whenever there was a spare minute. He made poppet dolls and small animals and anything else he fancied, and these small objects were often the only toys the children of these isolated homes knew.

The Presnells at work.

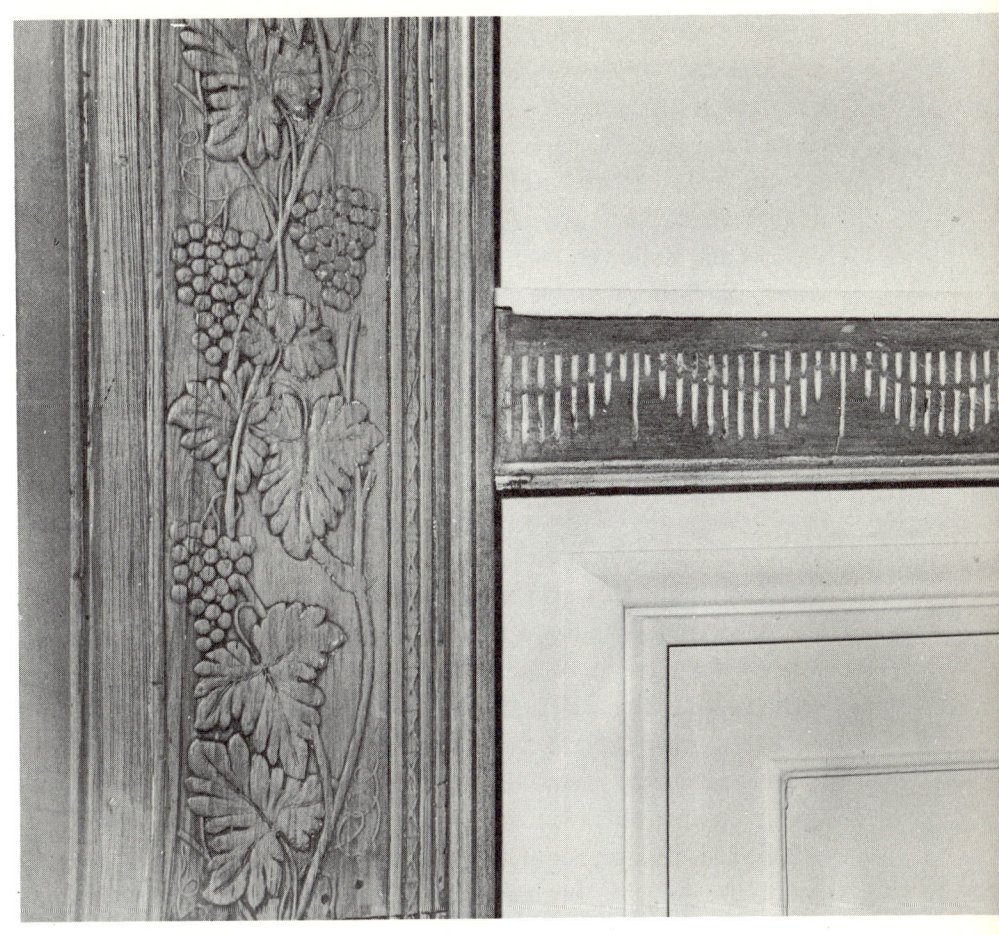

Carved molding.

Today's wood craftsmen, descendants in spirit and frequently in fact of the lonely pioneer, create carefully wrought articles from furniture to hand-turned forms of fruit, and bowls and trays that can be enjoyed as containers for other natural materials or for their beauty alone.

Asian peoples and particularly the Japanese have an innate feeling for natural wood. In their tiny eternally overpopulated islands, small segments of the natural world have always been precious. Until relatively recent times unusual trees were revered in their growing state. The art of wood carving flourished, just as in the West and wood was used for practical purposes, but an appreciation of natural wood was closely associated with the development of flower arrangement. A piece of barked wood was frequently placed vertically in the center of the classical rikka arrangement to meet symbolistic requirements. Later, a curving bare branch might be used in the ultra natural nageire arrangements for tea ceremony. Often a piece of bamboo wood was cut and hollowed to make a hanging vase for delicate arrangements of flowers and vines. In the classic Japanese house, a narrow-barked tree trunk, often slightly curved as it has grown, is still used to support the tokonoma alcove.

After World War II, when the rules of flower arrangement became less restrictive, the Japanese began to make imaginative use of natural wood in all kinds of arrangements. Bare branches were arranged with fresh or dried foliage, to emphasize the contrasts between the two natural materials. Curves of thorned branches complemented the delicacy of one or two pieces of fruit. The twisted angles of winter-dried vine stems were often added to simple arrangements of fresh flowers with intriguing visual results. Artistically formed pieces of driftwood were used as a background for fruits and vegetables in morimono arrangements. Even grotesquely contorted roots were cleaned and treated and pressed into service as containers and accessories.

Today when overpopulation threatens to obliterate the natural world, the West is beginning to understand and share some of the Japanese regard for the beauty of natural materials. Decorators and architects are emphasizing the use of natural wood in interiors. Driftwood in all its forms is being enjoyed as a unique natural accessory in home decorating.

Oriental arrangement of thorned branches with fruit.

Despite overtones of sandy shores, the term driftwood, in interior decorating, has come to include dead wood from the desert and inland waters, fallen tree limbs from the countryside and garden, gnarled roots, bare branches of interesting line, and twisted dried vines, as well as the offerings of the seashore. Decorative wood has been suggested as more precisely descriptive, but it has not gained wide acceptance. Weathered wood seems an all-embracing term, but driftwood continues to refer to natural wood of all shapes and sizes and textures, from everywhere.

For purposes of clarity in this chapter, we will refer to smaller branches and vines and roots and burls (cross-grained slices of wood) separately, using driftwood to mean any good-sized piece of dead wood from inland or coast. Natural wood will include all the above.

Sources of Natural Wood

The florist, together with the mail order sources listed at the end of this chapter, can provide a reasonably varied collection of wood. From these sources you can obtain treated and polished burls, Manzanita wood from the West Coast, and well-shaped unidentified pieces of driftwood. Some of these sources will have dried vines and bamboo wall vases as well. Long pieces of bamboo can be purchased quite reasonably from rug and carpet stores.

Driftwood Hunting

No matter where you live, however, collecting your own driftwood can be easy and fun. You'll be able to build a collection of distinctive shapes and textures fairly quickly. In time, you may find yourself looking for pieces of a particular kind of wood because you like its color or grain. If you hunt driftwood in the woods, you will probably become aware of the diversity of the tree barks. Some barks are rough, others smooth, some mottled, and still others shaggy. If you have never thought very much about it, you may not have noticed the distinctive forms of the different trees. Some species are tall and thrusting, others are perfectly rounded, and there are all types of angular and symmetrical variations in between.

You can collect natural wood at any time of the year, but

the best pickings are after a storm. For sheer exhilaration, try to go out early in the morning when the world is swept clean and the air is fresh. Look first for slender branches that have blown down in the garden or park or even an empty lot. In the woods look along the banks of lakes and streams where roots and driftwood dislodged by the storm can be found caught in crags and tiny coves. The seashore will yield its best after a storm too. At that time salt-cured wood that may have drifted downstream to the sea years before is washed ashore for your taking. Sometimes the pieces are so large and contain so many interesting blunted and twisted branches that a hand saw would be a useful piece of natural wood-hunting equipment.

The swamp and the desert both produce unique pieces of natural wood with marvelous decorating possibilities. Winter, when the climate is more reasonable and some of the native wildlife is sleeping, is the best time to forage these areas.

Sea-washed driftwood.

After the first hard frost, in most parts of our country, you can cut interesting curves and angles of dried vines from the countryside or garden. Morning Glory vines especially contort into unusual patterns. Decorative woods of garden trees and shrubs can be cut in late fall and used without further treatment, but some thought should be given to the shape of the tree after such pruning.

When you have gained a little experience in hunting for natural wood, you will begin to see the potential of unlikely branches and roots and driftwood that need only a little cleaning and judicious pruning to make them decoratively valuable.

Treating and Conditioning Driftwood

Most wood benefits from at least a quick rinse in clear water. Driftwood from inland sources will probably have to be washed in a pan of sudsy water and rinsed in clear, and then allowed to dry in the sun for a day or two. Heavily dirt-encrusted pieces of driftwood and roots should be soaked in sudsy water for an hour or two and then scrubbed with a heavy scrub brush. Use a toothbrush to clean out small ridges. Rinse the wood in clear water, and allow it to dry in the sun for about a week.

After wood has been cleaned and has dried thoroughly, take time to examine it. Cut out any damaged spots with a penknife and prune away obviously unwanted stubs and twigs. Then study it closely while you turn it in different positions to discover its best sides. Additional pruning may then be needed. The following chart shows how to improve the lines of various types of wood with thoughtful pruning.

Wood can be used with its bark or the bark may be removed. This will be academic for a piece that has weathered for a long time, but if you want to remove the bark of a newly fallen piece of wood, soak it for several hours in warm water and then scrape the bark away with a penknife.

Some roots and driftwood are improved with bleaching. This streaks the wood to a light gray color without destroying its natural appearance. It's easy to do, although results vary; some wood refuses to absorb bleach but experimenting is worthwhile. After the wood has been cleaned and pruned, submerge it in a solution

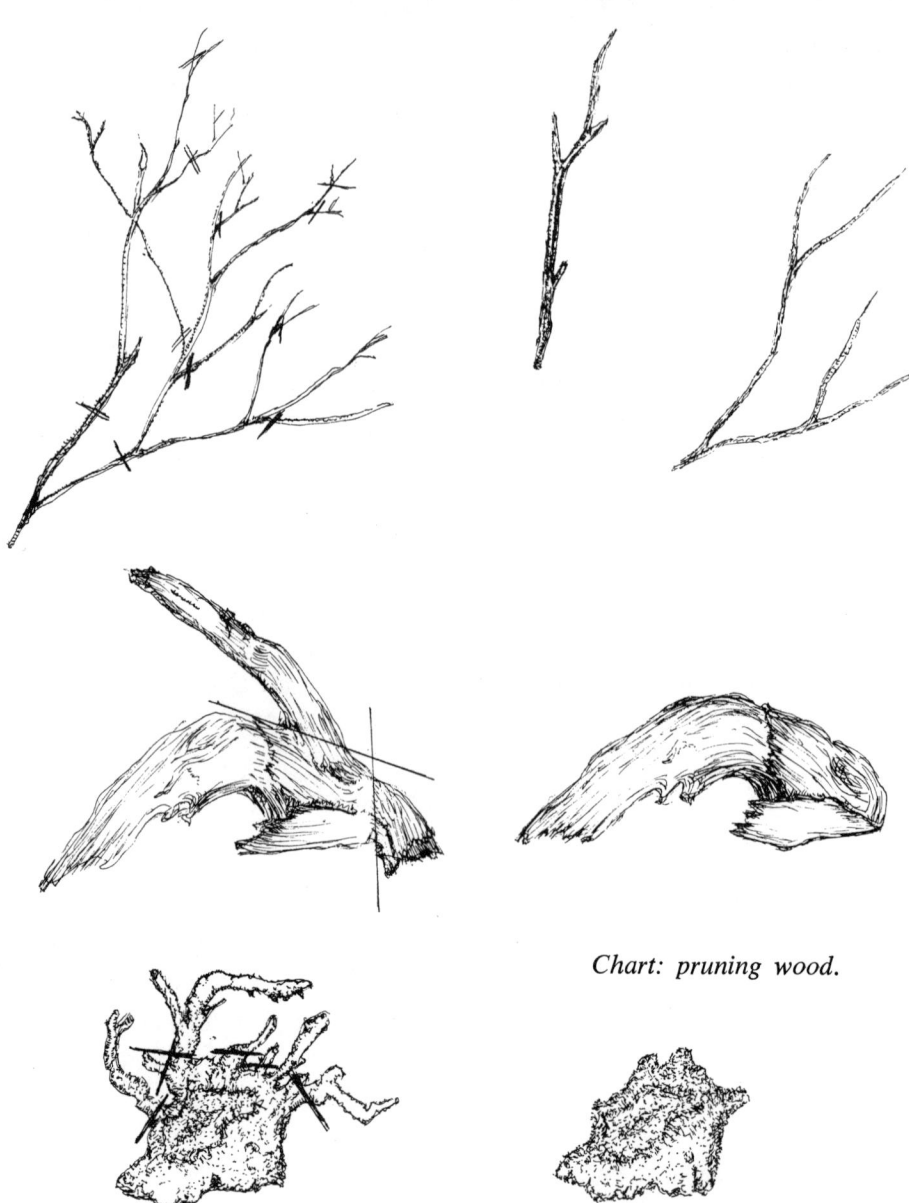

Chart: pruning wood.

of one part household bleach to two parts water. Leave the wood in the solution for forty-eight hours and then without rinsing allow the wood to dry in the sun for at least a week. Wood can be painted too, of course, but paint destroys its natural appearance as effectively as dyeing destroys a flower's beauty.

Slender branches and vines, because they are brittle, must be handled carefully. Generally they need little treatment. After some necessary pruning, rinse them in clear water and let them dry in an airy place. For formal interiors, you may want to spray branches and vines with a shiny, clear plastic spray.

Driftwood will have a more finished appearance if it is rubbed thoroughly with warm linseed oil after it has been cleaned and pruned. The oil can be poured into a saucer and warmed in the hot sun if you wish, or the bottle can be placed, opened, in hot water to warm. Pour the oil on a piece of cotton and rub it vigorously into the grain of the wood with some pressure for best results.

Natural wood can be stored in any convenient place until you are ready to use it; it is practically indestructible.

Decorative Ideas for Driftwood

Wood can be used decoratively in so many ways to add a new dimension of natural beauty to your home. The line of the wood, its texture and subtle coloring and your reactions to it, as well as the decorative needs of your home, will influence what you do with it.

Rugged pieces of driftwood seem made for informal areas. An interesting, weathered piece might be placed on end beside a fireplace in a den or family room. On a kitchen cabinet, a curve of gnarled driftwood can complement a grouping of fresh fruits and vegetables.

Bamboo can inspire innovative ideas. A friend of mine with imaginative ways has hung a four-foot length of bamboo in the entry of her traditionally furnished home. Good-sized openings have been cut between the joints of the bamboo trunk, and in these she has placed small Ivy and Philodendron and *Asparagus sprengeri* plants in their clay pots to provide a lovely cascade of green foliage down the side of the bamboo pole. Small holes were drilled in three places down the length of the back of the pole to receive large screw eyes which are used to hang the pole from heavy-duty picture-hanging fixtures. In summer this natural wood plant stand is moved outside to the screened porch where it softens the effect of a stone wall and adds vertical contrast to the rounded forms of hanging plants and floor-standing bouquets—a charming place to enjoy morning coffee with the lady of the house.

Bamboo trunk with plants.

Driftwood with stones.

Contemporary and some period interiors can be enhanced with a well-polished piece of driftwood of good line placed upright with a selection of polished stones, perhaps on a table or on the floor beside a grouping of plants. The simplicity and dramatic impact of wood used as natural sculpture are compatible with the most demanding surroundings.

Medium-sized curves of natural wood including Manzanita wood are decorative when hung in what might otherwise be a dull wall space. Use a drill to make a small hole in the back of the wood to receive a screw eye which can be hung from a picture-hanging fixture. You can enjoy the lines of the wood alone or place a small wall-hung vase behind it to hold glycerinized foliage or fresh flowers. I've seen this same idea used to decorate the exterior of a small Cape Cod cottage. Behind a weathered piece of driftwood a hanging basket holds a jar of water. In this, the pleasant white-haired lady who lives in the house places tiny bouquets of garden flowers all summer. At Christmas time, Evergreens and Holly branches curve around the driftwood, and for some of the winter the driftwood hangs starkly unadorned in keeping with the general appearance of the season.

Flowers and foliage with driftwood.

On a dining-room table or a sideboard in an informal room, a curve of driftwood is lovely in the fall of the year arranged with dried Strawflowers and Gourds. The Gourds need only to be piled attractively in the curve of the wood, and the Strawflowers with stems cut very short can be placed on top and between the Gourds. In season fresh flowers and foliage can be arranged with the driftwood. Place a small bowl of water in the curve of the wood. You may want a piece of crumpled floral wire inside the container to hold the fresh plant material. Arrange the foliage first to form a frame for the flowers and to hide the container. Add flowers in among the leaves. The foliage will last for a long time and the flowers can be replaced as they fade. Be sure to keep the water level constant.

For winter elegance try a bare winter branch combined with a branch of needled Evergreen. Prune both branches to achieve an open effect. A block container about six inches square is a good size and shape for this arrangement. Anchor a needlepoint holder with clay to the floor of the container. Condition the Evergreen branches (see Chapter Four) and cut the branch ends at a slant. Both branches should be about three times the height of the container. Arrange them close together and stiffly upright. Add water; the effect is stark and dramatic.

A bundle of long switchy branches placed in a handsome floor-standing vase is marvelous for filling an empty corner. Gather ten or twelve long, straight, leafless branches from a tall shrub. Prune away any cross twigs. You want long whiplike lines. Place a piece of crumpled chicken wire in the bottom of the container and add a stone for stabilizing weight. Then, holding the bunch tightly together, lower it into the vase. Catch the branch bottoms in the floral wire, then let the bunch fall casually open. To be effective, the height of the branches should be about twice the height of your

Long switchy branches in floor-standing vase.

Root with fresh flowers.

container. If the container is tall enough, the bouquet will extend far up the wall, perhaps three quarters of the way to the ceiling.

Roots have such a craggy weathered look about them that they seem to belong in rustic informal rooms. Some roots can act as containers for fresh flowers, if a small jar stuffed with water-soaked Oasis is placed in a likely indentation. If your root does not provide a handy place for a container, just put the jar behind the root and use vines and long-stemmed flowers that can be pulled forward a bit over the root. A Morning Glory vine that has a good number of unopened buds on the vine would be attractive. The flowers last only for a day, but the buds will continue to open on successive days to contrast delicately with the sturdy root.

Combine dried vines with fresh or dried flowers in an oriental-style bouquet and you will create an arrangement that is appropriate for almost any style interior. Just anchor a needlepoint holder to the floor of a low container with floral clay. Place three vines curving upward and add four short-stemmed flowers and some short sprigs of foliage low and within the frame of the dried vines. Especially nice on a coffee table.

If you need height on a table top, perhaps to balance a tall lamp or high standing piece of furniture, try an arrangement of fairly thick branches pruned severely into straight and angular lines and cut off bluntly at the top. This arrangement is dramatic enough for a living room or sufficiently casual for a den. Just choose a vertical container to complement the interior. Here again the branches should be at least twice the height of the container to be effective.

Miniatures

Miniatures of driftwood are delightful and easy to make. A twig from the end of a Manzanita or other slender branch can impersonate a large piece of driftwood. The tiny branch can be arranged with tiny berries such as Bittersweet berries and a few pieces of dried herb leaves, all held in place with a dab of floral clay. A small piece of wood in a low container combined with a few dried Starflowers is a delightful miniature bouquet with an oriental feeling. Other miniatures can be adopted from the suggestions given for full-sized decorating effects or from your own imagination. Enough perhaps for a shadow box filled with permanent miniatures to fill a bare wall space.

Mail Order Sources:

Garden Club Products
Mapes' Garden Center
Route 1, Kennebunk,
Me. 04043

Unusual hand-rubbed wood bases. Bamboo "rafts." Catalogue.

Boycan's Floral Arts
1052 E. State St.
Sharon, Penna. 16146

Manzanita wood. Camphor wood slabs. Catalogue.

Gay Dolphin Gift Cove
Myrtle Beach, S.C. 29577

All kinds of sea-washed driftwood, as well as sea shells. No catalogue.

Chapter Eight

Pine Cones

If you think Christmas when you see pine cones, do think again, because they are much more versatile. When used with imagination and combined with other natural materials they become fascinating year-round accessories for the home.

The form of the pine cone has inspired artists and craftsmen for centuries. It has been chiseled in stone and carved in wood. As mentioned in Chapter Six, the pine cone, along with other natural plant forms was the motif of sculpture and bas-relief executed by the talented Della Robbia family of fifteenth-century Italy.

Today, craftswomen of the Southern Highland Handicraft Guild and other crafts groups use the pine cone to fashion lovely wreaths and swags and other ·decorative articles, as pictured on the opposite page. The women gather their own pine cones and acorns and similar natural materials, which they call wood pretties. Some of the designs and ideas they use are their own, others come from interested people from the "outside" who suggest articles that can compete successfully in the urban market place. An espaliered pine cone tree is one of the more sophisticated and exquisitely crafted articles that I have seen. To watch the craftswomen intently and skillfully at work is a rewarding experience. The story of handicrafts in all parts of our country is fascinating. Perhaps because I am familiar with the Southern Highland Handicraft Guild, of Asheville, North Carolina, I find its background most heart-warming. Its existence is the result of trust and faith and giving, the realization of the desire of a few people to help many who wanted to help themselves. It was necessary for the mountain people to overcome their natural shyness and distrust of those who were different in speech and manners. But the teachers and social workers who came from outside the mountains, came with respect for the character and human dignity of the highlanders. From tentative beginnings

Two handicrafts as practiced in my part of the country: H. and T. Pottery, Asheboro, North Carolina.

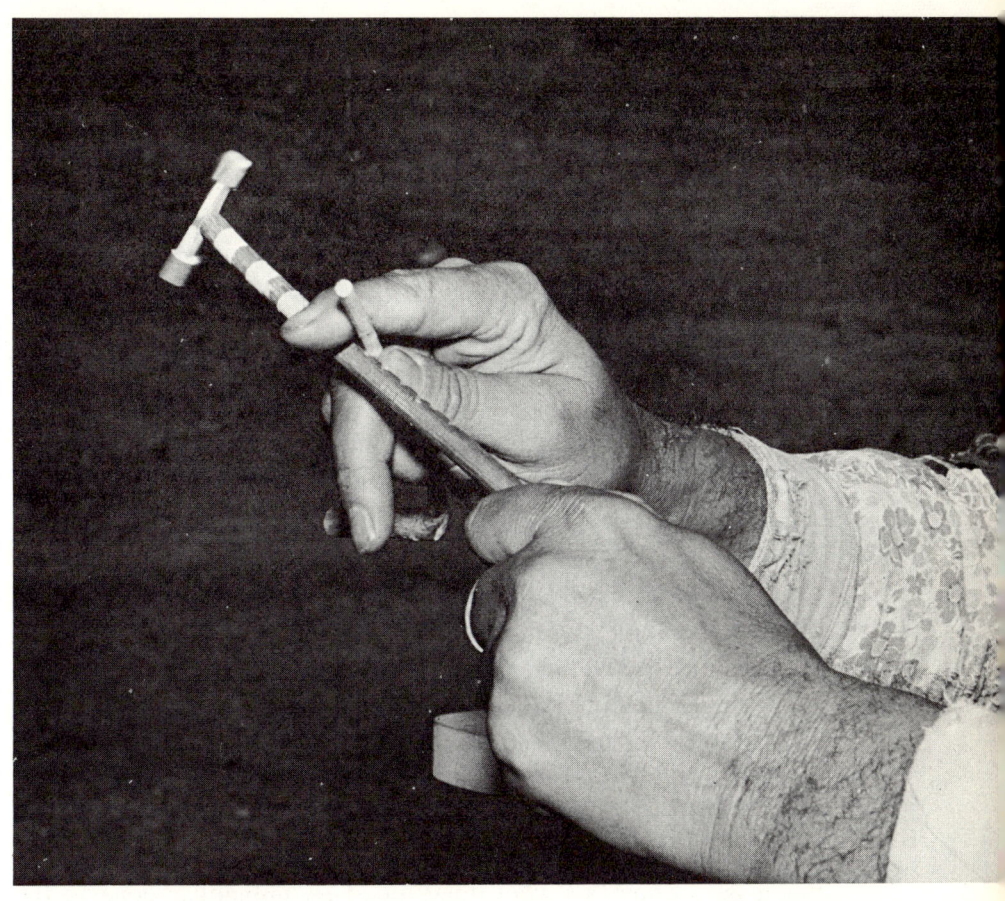

Gee haw whimmy diddle handcrafted toy.

the venture has prospered into an efficient organization functioning for the benefit of its continually expanding list of members. The complete story has been beautifully told by Allen Eaton, in his book *Handicrafts of the Southern Highlands,* listed in the reading list at the end of this book. Do become acquainted with the crafts of your own area, including Indian crafts. Handcrafted objects including pine-cone accessories can add a unique decorative accent to your home.

An interest in pine cones, as with other crafts, opens many related avenues of interest. If you have just a passing acquaintance with needled Evergreens now, you may find yourself acquiring an ability to recognize the many different varieties. The trees that produce cones are as varied as the pine cones themselves. Hemlocks, Spruces, Firs, Larches, along with the Pines like Lodgepole, Loblolly, Sugar, and Longleaf are just a few of the conifers. Some trees, like many Spruces, have rather drooping branches and short needles. Balsam Firs have a pyramidal, Christmas-tree shape. The branches of some are covered with needles, and others like the Pines produce needles in tufts. The Longleaf Pine has needles over a foot long, Hemlock needles are only about a half inch long. A few trees like the Larches have feathery needles but most needles are stiff, and the barks of all the trees are slightly different and provide another means of identification.

Trees reach cone-bearing age at different times—some in a very few years, others take much longer, and many cone-producing trees do not produce cones every year. Some cones take several years to mature from an unscaled rather inconspicuous beginning to the fully developed cone we use for decorative projects. Hemlock cones are about the smallest cones, usually less than an inch. The largest cones are produced by the Sugar Pine and are frequently over a foot long. Surprisingly the cones of the giant Sequoias of the West Coast are only a few inches long, and those of the Redwoods are even smaller.

The curious forms of the pine cone seem irresistible. The impulse to pick up and carry home unusual cones is probably universal. One imagines that the colonists and the early western pioneers might have done this when they found an unfamiliar cone in the then virgin forests, perhaps carrying it into their rough cabins for casual and unconsidered decoration.

Collecting Pine Cones

The best time to collect pine cones is in the early fall, late September or early October. Most serious craftsmen will not use fallen cones, but I have bruised and torn my hands trying to cut them from the branches and of course a ladder is needed to reach very high branches so I gather fallen cones. You may take your choice. You will need a sharp pair of metal clippers to cut the varieties I am familiar with from the trees. If you decide to gather fallen cones, check them carefully for rotting spots and discard those that are not perfect. The cones should be clear in color and not at all weathered-looking. If you are collecting from the ground, go several times in the fall to find newly fallen cones. Some trees do not drop cones too readily but a sufficient number do to make this a practical way of gathering them.

If you cannot collect your own pine cones, the mail order sources at the end of the chapter can supply you with a great variety. In fact it is interesting, even when you gather your own, to send for unusual cones not to be found near home.

Drying and Conditioning Cones

Clean cones that are sticky with pitch with a rag dipped in turpentine, then place them in the sun and air for a few days. Cones open fully and stay opened only if they are completely dry. It can be disconcerting to find improperly dried cones closing tight in moist weather and ruining a decorative effect you have spent some time creating. The best place to dry the cones is in the oven. Preheat your oven to 250 degrees and leave it at this temperature for five minutes, then turn it off. Lay the cones on a rack in the heated oven with the door closed for five minutes. Don't be dismayed by the cracking sounds some cones make as they dry. They won't explode. If there is any pitch on the cones, it will drip, so it is best to put a flat pan on the shelf beneath them. When the cones are dried, let them cool and then spray them thoroughly, inside the scales and all over, with a clear plastic spray. The spray is available in either matte or glossy finish, and the choice is up to you.

Cutting Pine Cone Flowers

You will probably want to cut the cones into "flowers" and to wire them for some decorating projects. Both procedures are fairly simple but require some patience and practice. To cut the pine cones, you'll need a good sharp pair of wire cutters from the hardware store. Now hold the pine cone in one hand and the clippers in the other. Push the open clippers in as far as they will go between the scales about three rows up from the bottom of the cone. Push the clippers gently but with strength and cut at the same time. You can frequently cut through small cones on the first trial. To cut larger cones, like the Sugar Pine cone, push and cut as far as you can from one side, then turn the cone and push and cut again. Rotate the cone until you have made at least four cuts which should

Cutting pine cone flowers.

separate it into two pieces. The cut side looks like a single-petaled flower. Turn it over and it resembles a multi-petaled Zinnia. You will be able to cut more than one flower from large cones.

To wire a pine cone and pine cone flowers, you'll need a #22 floral wire, available at most florists and flower arranging stores, and from mail order sources listed at the end of the chapters. Floral wire is sold in strands about a foot long. Slip this length of wire around the core of the cone or the cone flower, placing it above the first row of scales. Pull both ends together and twist. The wire will extend out one side. Just pull it back under the cone or flower and cut it to the length you need. If you find you need a longer stem,

Wiring a pine cone.

twist additional wire around the first stem, then cover with brown floral tape. Start at the top of the wire stem underneath the cone and wind the tape around and around until the stem is completely covered.

Accessories Made from Pine Cones

Among the simplest and yet most appealing accessories are baskets filled with pine cones with perhaps the tops of some stalks of wheat. You can use many different kinds of baskets. A Willow wastebasket for instance is charming filled to the top with large pine cones and accented with a scattering of smaller pine cones and a few sprigs of glycerinized Shallon (Lemon Leaf) tucked in between the cones. Try it, floor standing, in an informal family or living room through most of the year. At Christmas time, tuck in sprigs of Holly, putting their stems in water-filled water picks, tucked out of sight beneath the cones. The same idea can be used in a period room perhaps using a boughpot container to hold the cones. This is attractive in an empty fireplace. Large low baskets with handles, the kind one associates with ladies gathering flowers

Willow basket filled with pine cones and sprigs of foliage.

from the garden, can be piled with cones and some pomander balls (see Chapter Nine) and a scattering of Strawflowers, then placed on a counter top or shelf. Use these same ideas for smaller baskets that can go on side tables or desks, changing the Strawflowers to Starflowers for the smaller versions.

A more finished-looking basket of pine cones and pine cone flowers can be made with just a little effort. A round basket about six inches high, at the top of the handle, is a good size to use. Cut a piece of Styrofoam to fill the basket and anchor it in the basket with Styrofoam glue or floral clay. Cover the foam with sheet moss from a florist or mail order service. Cut the moss a little larger than the rim of the basket and put it over the Styrofoam, tucking the ends down inside the basket. To create an overflowing effect for the size basket mentioned above, you'll need about eight medium-sized pine cone flowers and about a dozen small, one to one and a half inch, pine cones. Cut the pine cone flowers from medium-sized pine cones following the method suggested earlier in the chapter. Wire stems to the cones and cone flowers, then wire wooden picks (available at many florists and from mail order) to the wired stems. Now push the wooden picks, attached to the pine cone flowers, down through the moss into the Styrofoam until the top is fairly well covered. Then place the small pick-wired pine cones in between the pine cone flowers. Wire additional wooden picks to your choice of small sprigs of dried glycerinized foliage or perhaps tiny bouquets of beige (natural) Starflowers which would complement the brown of the cones beautifully. Place these finishing touches here and there among the cones. When you are pleased

Basket of pine cones and pine cone flowers.

with the effect, spray the entire arrangement, basket and all, with a glossy clear plastic spray. These little baskets are delightful accessories almost everywhere, even in the bathroom. At Christmas

Bouquet of long-stemmed pine cone flowers.

time, you can substitute fresh greens for the dried foliage or Starflowers, in keeping with the season.

An exceptionally good-looking accessory can be made from very large pine cone flowers. You will need about a dozen pine cone flowers measuring about two inches across after they are cut. Use the single-petaled side and wire the cone flowers as directed before. Then attach an additional strand of floral wire to provide a stem at least a foot long. Now, hopefully, you will have some dried wheat or barley or other hollow-stemmed dried material at hand. If you do, cut off the tops and slide the pine cone flower's wire stem inside the dried stem. The effect is very "natural" looking. If you don't have any hollow stems available, cover the long wire stem with brown floral tape as described before. Now with all these unusual brown flowers ready, decide where they are to go and select a tall vase that is compatible with the other furnishings in the room. A stoneware crock might be nice in an informal area. A tall ivory ceramic container would be appropriate for a contemporary room. If you can obtain it, fill your container to a depth of four or five inches with sand and place the flower stems in this. The heads should extend about four inches above the rim of the vase, in a casual unarranged fashion.

Medium-sized to small pine cones are attractive arranged with Gourds on a pewter tray or perhaps in a low wide bowl. It's very easily done. But for an added touch of fragrance, you might want to put a sachet of Pine in the container first. Then arrange the Gourds so that the sachet is hidden. Short sprigs of Dock tucked about the necks of the Gourds are a nice accent, and you can add a scattering of acorns or Sweet Gum balls as a final fillip.

An eye-catching winter bouquet that is as appropriate to a formal period interior as it is to a more casual surrounding can be made with a branch or two of longleaf Pine placed upright in a tall good-looking vase. The branch will look best if it is about twice the height of the container. Beside it place two or three pine cones from the same tree. Make regional variations, with needled Evergreen branches from your own area and their cones. This is a lovely accessory for a chest perhaps in an entrance hall.

Medium-sized to small pine cones with long stems added can be arranged with branches of glycerinized foliage, perhaps Pittosporum or Aucuba in bouquets of any size, from table top to tall. Use them on side tables or chests or shelves anywhere in the house, choosing a container that is appropriate in size as well as style to the place where it will be displayed. Crumpled floral wire will hold the arrangement and you may want to add a stone to stabilize a tall container.

Wreaths

Christmas wreaths made entirely of pine cones are becoming very popular, because they are naturally lovely and permanent. Other wreaths like the Della Robbia are handsome but can be enjoyed for just a season. Wreaths take a little time and patience to make, but the natural handcrafted effect is well worth the effort. Results are most satisfactory, if you use a wreath base purchased at the florist. These are usually covered with sheet moss. The twenty-inch size is right for most front doors. These bases keep their shape well, and the wired cones and pine cone flowers or other materials can be attached very easily. Styrofoam bases are not satisfactory for a large wreath. Wire bases can be purchased quite reasonably but I don't recommend them. They are just circles composed of perhaps six wire rings. They must be covered with burlap which has been cut into strips and then wrapped around and around the rings. Wire coat hangers

Making a pine cone wreath.

that have been forced into a ring form are also used occasionally as a base. Since the wreath takes time and patience to make and is a genuinely creative effort, in my opinion it is best to use a professional florist's wreath base. With your wreath base on hand, you can decide on a design. A Della Robbia wreath made with Evergreens and varnished fruit (see Chapter Six), as well as small pine cones and nuts, is lovely but perishable. Continuously freezing weather will discolor the fruit. However, if you decide to make one, cover your wreath with short branches of needled Evergreen or Box or foliage that is available in your area and fairly long lasting. Condition the foliage as described in Chapter Four.

Lash the foliage to the wreath base, encircling both base and foliage with floral wire and pulling it tight. Twist-close the wire on the underside of the wreath. Choose small fruits—little red Apples and some citrus fruits are a good choice. Wire two wooden picks together and poke one deep inside each fruit. Now arrange the fruits on the wreath, rather casually, pushing the picks into the wreath base. Remember that the wreath is convex and must have some fruit on either side for an attractive appearance. Add wired nuts and small pine cones in among the fruit to complete the arrangement. One word of caution: Do not make this wreath too long before Christmas. The varnished fruits will stay fresh for about three weeks in a moderate climate with temperatures several degrees above freezing.

A wreath of Boxwood, fruit, and pine cones in Colonial Williamsburg.

You can make pine cone wreaths with or without foliage. If you are using foliage, lash it to the wreath base as described above and push pick-wired pine cones and pine cone flowers into the wreath base on top of the foliage.

A wreath made from an assortment of pine cones, some

whole, some cut into flowers, is delightful and of course, if stored carefully, it can be used year after year. An important question: How many pine cones are needed? Cones vary so much in size that it's difficult to be precise, but for a twenty-inch wreath base, you will need about 140 pine cones of the Loblolly variety. These are about four or five inches long. Well over 200 smaller cones would be needed for the same size wreath. A wreath made with several varieties of pine cones is interesting. Pine cone flowers are very decorative placed here and there among the larger cones. Nuts, acorns, and Sweet Gum balls all add a touch of individuality to the wreath. These small materials will need a hole drilled through them to hold the wired pick. Now to start, have your wreath base ready and wire wooden picks to the pine cones and pine cone flowers and other materials. Start with the largest cones and place them on the wreath, firmly pushing the pick into the base. Add smaller cones in between the large ones, filling the inner and outer sides of the convex wreath form first. On top, add the cut pine cone flowers and any other touches, like nuts or acorns. When you think you have finished, there will probably still be some holes. Check carefully and fill in any spaces with the small cones. When you are completely satisfied, spray the entire wreath several times with glossy, clear plastic spray.

Plaques for Wall Decorations

Pine cone flowers arranged with other dried materials on a plaque make a handsome wall decoration. A simple dark Walnut frame would be compatible with the natural materials and give the plaque a finished appearance. Choose the frame first. If it has no backing, a piece of plywood to fit the back will do. In addition, you'll need a piece of hardware cloth, as well as a piece of coarse-weave linen or burlap, both a little larger than the backing, for a background. Decide on the design and the materials you are going to use. It's easiest to try out several designs choosing from Wheat or Dock, perhaps Pussy Willow stems, glycerinized Ivy or Eucalyptus, Strawflowers, and of course pine cone flowers. Have your pine cone flowers wired and have thin floral wire at hand to attach the other materials to the plaque. Now cover the hardware cloth with the burlap or linen and arrange the longest piece of natural material on it. With a toothpick, put a drop of clear glue under the plant material at strategic points. Then take the thin floral wire and place it around the dried materials in several places, trying to keep it hidden by perhaps a small leaf or catkin. Pull the ends of the wire through the cloth to the back and twist the two ends together close to the back of the hardware cloth. Put all your material in place in this manner, following your design. If any material does not seem firmly anchored to the background, dab a small drop of glue beneath the part that is hanging free. When everything is in place, leave it for a few hours or overnight and then place it on the picture frame backing. To do this, lay the backing on the table, place the design, which is firmly in place on the background, on top of the backing. The cloth background should overlap the backing on all four sides. Fold this material over the frame backing and staple it to the backing. Then place the plaque in the frame and hang it wherever a bare wall needs a decorative accent.

Miniatures

Pine cone miniatures are as fetching as those made with other natural materials. Most of the suggestions for decorative cone ideas can be used to make tiny look alikes. Hemlock cones or similar small cones can be used to carry out the design. A tiny wreath is very easy to make and would be a delightful Christmas favor. Use a miniature Styrofoam base and the finest floral wire to attach the cones to the base. Most small pine cones will prove too fragile to cut into flowers, but do experiment with what is available in your area. Miniature basket arrangements can be made in much the same way as the larger baskets except that the cones will probably be tiny whole cones. Privet berries or Bayberries would add an interesting accent.

Mail Order Sources:

Garden Club Products
Mapes' Garden Center
Kennebunk, Me. 04043

Variety of pine cones. Catalogue.

Boycan's Floral Arts
1052 E. State St.
Sharon, Penna. 16146

Wire frames for wreaths. Pine cones. Wired pine cones. Catalogue.

Western Tree Cones
1925 Brooklane
Corvallis, Ore. 97330

Pine cones. Sweet gum balls. Cut cone flowers. Catalogue.

Floral Art
P. O. Box 394, Highland Sta.
Springfield, Mass. 01109

Water picks. Wired wood picks. Clippers. Spray. Some cones. Catalogue.

Chapter Nine

Fragrance

To awaken in the mountains on a cool spring morning with the sharp clean smell of the wooded slopes in the air is an exhilarating experience. To have this fragrance always in our own homes is to refresh the spirits with a constant reminder of the natural world.

Every home has its own atmosphere, a delightful or depressing indication of the values and style of the people within. In some homes there is first of all the furious smell of furniture polish and disinfectant. In others it is the mustiness of dust and unswept corners. Some homes have the stale remembrance of a thousand dinners lingering in the air, while others seem to speak of closed-off rooms and dried-up memories. Sometimes a synthetic scented deodorizer obliterates the character of a house completely the way cheap perfume smothers the personality of its wearer. But some homes do have the fragrance of a springtime morning all through the year. It's not too difficult to manage.

The appreciation of natural fragrance is an ancient pleasure. The Egyptians scattered Rose petals underfoot and delighted in the fragile scent. Some Egyptians of those early centuries had Rose petals sewed into their pallets, presumably to provide fragrant dreams. The Romans used Lavender and other scents in their baths, and in ancient Greece, men and women alike enjoyed perfumed unguents so precisely that they used a different scent on each part of their body. The Greeks placed pots of flowers chosen for their fragrance in their small enclosed gardens, believing that the scents would prevent disease. They favored the herb Ambrosia for scenting cloth, using it in much the same way that, centuries later, the Victorians used Lavender. The Victorians incidentally believed that the odor of Lavender would dissipate passion, which may explain why it was such a popular sachet in that repressed era.

During the Middle Ages and later, fragrant herbs were strewn over the freshly swept floors of homes and churches to ward off disease and refresh the spirit. These strewing herbs, especially Camomile and Thyme, were often turf cuttings. It is still possible, if one wishes, to have a small lawn of Thyme and, recalling Shakespeare's "I know a bank where the wild thyme grows," to throw oneself luxuriously into it and fragrantly dream away at least part of a summer's day.

In seventeenth-century England and probably before, it was the custom to tie the herb Sweet Woodruff into small bunches which were hung from the rafters in summer to dry. The characteristic odor of freshly mown hay was found cooling and refreshing on hot days. Colonial settlers continued the pleasant custom in America. If you have a big old-fashioned country kitchen with rafters, you might want to do the same. Sweet Woodruff, by the way, is the same herb that is used in Germany and in German restaurants here to flavor the delightful spring wine called *Maiwein*.

Herb Bowls

The aroma of dried herbs, reminiscent of farmlands and meadows, seems most appropriate to informal areas like kitchens and family rooms and country cottages. If you do not have rafters from which to hang bunches of drying herbs, you might want to make an herb bowl. This is just a covered bowl of one or

Medieval still room—print from "Le Proprietaire des Choses" by Bartholamaeus Angelicus, Paris, 1510.

several dried herbs whose fragrance has been made enduring with a fixative. Whenever the cover of the bowl is lifted, the fresh sweet natural odors refresh the spirits. Pint-sized covered casseroles make charming herb bowls or, if your supply of herbs is limited, small jam pots can be used. Use leaves from herbs in your window garden or outdoor garden. If you have neither, top quality herbs from your grocer's spice shelf can be used. They must be fresh. They should have a slightly pungent odor. If they smell pleasantly of sun-dried hay, they are not fresh. Camomile, Mint, Thyme, Rosemary, Sweet Woodruff, Basil, and Dill are a few of the herbs that can be used. But sniff about and find the ones that please you most. Rosemary and Mint are a particularly pleasant combination.

To Make an Herb Bowl

Materials needed

A flat piece of screening
Support for the screen
A glass jar
Orrisroot from the druggist
A decorative covered bowl, jam pot, or teapot

Procedure

To dry herbs:

Place the screening on the support which can be a drying rack or two bricks or anything that will permit a circulation of air below and above the screen.

Gather herb foliage on a dry day in the morning as soon as the dew has disappeared.

Strip the leaves from the stems.

Place herb leaves in a single layer on the screening so that they do not touch.

Allow to remain in a dim dry place until completely dry.

Time: from five days to two weeks. The leaves will feel like corn flakes when dry.

Note: If you are using dried herbs from the grocer, start here:

Place the dried herb leaves in a jar.

Add two tablespoons orrisroot to each pint: two cups of leaves.

Mix thoroughly.

Cover the jar tightly and place in a dim dry place.

Turn and shake jar every few days.

After three weeks, pour the herb mixture into decorative covered bowls.

The fragrance of the herbs will usually last for several seasons. Leave the bowl uncovered frequently to enjoy the delightful odor. If your bowl is large enough, run your fingers through the leaves occasionally to stir them and enjoy the rising scent; otherwise stir the mixture with a small spoon from time to time.

Potpourri

Potpourri is another fragrance mixture, similar to but more complex than an herb bowl. Basically it is a combination of fragrant flower petals and spices to which a variety of other exotically scented materials can be added. Potpourri enjoyed its greatest popularity in the French courts of the sixteenth and seventeenth centuries. Rare spices were beginning to trickle in from abroad and many delightful fragrances were evolved. The

Herb bowl.

name potpourri has come to mean a mixture, but the French freely translate as "rotten jar." It is from the Spanish *olla podrida,* which is simply a stew. There are two methods of making a potpourri, one moist and the other dry. It is the moist method which may have inspired the name, for it goes though a stage of being a mess of rotting petals before it comes into its own. The dry method is the one we will consider here.

At the height of its popularity, special jars were made for potpourri mixtures. These often had two covers, one perforated and the other solid to fit over the perforated cover when the fragrance was not being enjoyed. If you have collecting instincts, these charming jars can, with some perseverance, be found in antique shops. Any attractive covered jar or pot or bowl that is appropriate to your home can be used for potpourri however.

When royalty was the rule almost every queen had her favorite recipe for the sweet jar. It's perhaps a good idea to start with a very simple mixture with small amounts of ingredients. The ingredients in the following recipe can be doubled if you wish.

Simple Potpourri

Recipe for simple potpourri

½ cup dried fragrant Rose petals
½ cup dried flower petals for bulk
2 tablespoons orrisroot
½ tablespoon each Nutmeg, Cinnamon, crushed Lemon peel

Materials needed

Screening
Support for screening, see previous directions for herb bowl
Three medium-sized glass jars with covers
A decorative jar or bowl with cover

Method

Place screening so that there is a circulation above and below it.
Gather fragrant Roses and flowers for bulk just before the flowers reach full bloom.

Pick on a dry day just as soon as the dew has disappeared.

Remove petals from flowers.

Spread the petals in a single layer on the screening.

Place in a dim dry area.

Check after four or five days.

The flowers will feel very crisp if dry.

If they are not completely dry, they will mold.

Place dried rose petals in one jar, petals for bulk in a separate jar.

When you have collected ½ cup of each, continue in this way:

- Place some of the Rose petals in the bottom of the jar.
- Add some bulk petals, sprinkle with a little of the orrisroot.
- Continue until all the petals and orrisroot have been used.
- Add spices and citrus peel at the end.
- Stir gently.
- Cover the jar tightly.
- Place in a dark dry place.

Turn and shake the jar occasionally.

After a month the mixture is ready to use.

Pour it into your potpourri jar and enjoy.

Dried Lavender flowers and dried Rose petals are commonly used in potpourri because they retain their fragrance better than most flowers. The Apothecary (*Rosa gallica officinalis*) and the Damask Roses have the best fragrance retention. Many Roses have little or no fragrance, or the petals may lose their fragrance when dry. These, along with other flowers that lack fragrance, can be used to provide bulk in the potpourri mixture. Lavender flowers should be gathered just before full bloom. Many old recipes use equal amounts of Lavender flowers and Rose petals. This makes a pleasant fragrance, but the spiciness of the Lavender has a tendency to overpower the Rose. The fixative orrisroot is just the powdered root of the Florentine Iris. If you are a purist you can grow it and powder it yourself with a mortar and pestle, I presume. Orrisroot is available through your druggist. He may have to order it for you, but it is quite inexpensive. Some herbs and spices that you do not or cannot grow are available from the grocer. Choose top quality, absolutely fresh products. Citrus peels are shaved from the fruit and dried exactly like flower petals. Any exotic ingredients mentioned in this section as well as dried Rose and Lavender petals are available by mail order if not from your druggist or grocer.

A seventeenth-century French pomander made from silver.

Personal Potpourri Mixtures

It's fun to experiment and concoct your own personal potpourri. Essentially potpourri mixture is made up of these parts:

> Dried fragrant flower petals, at least half the total bulk. You can use fragrant flower petals for the total bulk, but it takes a long time to collect them.
>
> Dried flower petals with little or no fragrance, not more than half the total bulk.
>
> Fixatives—more than one can be used.
>
> Blenders: Spices and herbs of your choosing.
>> Citrus peels, fragrant barks, woods, and roots.

To this basic mixture the following can be added:

> Additional fixative to deepen the fragrance.
>
> Concentrated oils to enhance the fragrance.

Ingredients for Potpourri

> Flowers for fragrance:
>> Rose petals, Lavendar petals, Orange blossoms, Carnation petals.
>
> Flowers for bulk:
>> Calendula, Strawflowers, Elder flowers, Roses without fragrance, and many others.
>
> Blenders:
>
> Spices and herbs:
>> Angelica, Anise, Mint, Rosemary, Thyme, Tonka, Vanilla bean, Cinnamon, Nutmeg, Mace, Cardamom, Cloves, Caraway, Rose Geranium leaves, Lemon Verbena.
>
> Citrus peel and barks and woods and seeds:
>> Lemon, Lime, Orange peels; Celery seed, Cedar wood, Eucalyptus, Gingerroot, Sandalwood, Sassafras.
>
> Fixatives: orrisroot, calamus root, ambergris, civet, vetiver.

Fragrant oils: There are a great number but some that are most generally useful are: Mimosa, Lime, Rose Geranium, Wisteria, Sandalwood, Bitter Almond, Orange blossom, Rose, and Lavender.

Elaborate Potpourri Mixtures

A more elaborate potpourri with more body and depth to its fragrance can be made using these ingredients:

    1 cup dried fragrant Rose petals
    ½ cup dried Carnation petals
    ¼ cup dried petals for bulk
    ¼ cup Lemon Verbena leaves
    1 tablespoon each, Mace, Rosemary, Cloves
    1 teaspoon oil of Rose Geranium
    4 tablespoons orrisroot
    1 tablespoon tonka

Mix together following directions given for simple potpourri.

Sachet

Sachet, little bags of fragrance, can be made from potpourri mixtures or simply from fragrant flower petals which have been sprinkled with orrisroot in the proportion of two tablespoons to one cup of petals and allowed to "fix" for three weeks or more in a tightly covered jar placed in a dim dry place. Lavender is

the traditional sachet for linens because of its fresh spicy fragrance. Sachets can also be made from herbs such as those used in the herb bowl or from any other fragrances you enjoy. Rose Geranium leaves or Lemon Verbena are delightful. A sachet that is practical as well as pleasant is made from Southernwood, an old-fashioned herb noted for its ability to drive away moths. The

Rosemary.

leaves are dried and processed in the same manner as leaves for the herb bowl.

Very simple sachet bags can be made from fine cotton or linen. Cut a six-inch square of material and hem it all around. Now put two or three tablespoons of the sachet mixture of your choice in the center of the square. Bring up all four corners and tie with a satin ribbon. Leave a loop of ribbon if you will want to hang the sachet from a hook or hanger.

Balsam Pillows

The Balsam pillow is a rather robust Pine sachet, which used to be a great favorite at souvenir stands at summer resorts. Directions should probably start with the advice: First find a Balsam tree. If you live where they grow, it is easy; if not, you can experiment with any fragrant pine needle.

To Make a "Balsam" Pillow:

Pick new growth of fragrant pine needles at the tips of the branches of the tree.

Strip needles from the branches and lay on fine mesh screening to dry.

There must be a circulation of air above and below the screen.

Check after one week.

The needles should feel dry; if not, allow to dry longer.

Then place in a jar with two tablespoons salt to one cup of needles.

Allow to "fix" for three weeks, turning and shaking the jar occasionally.

If you wish, you can add 1 tablespoon cedar bark and 1 teaspoon oil of pine to enhance the fragrance.

Bags for pine needles should be made from close-weave burlap or other heavy material. You can make the little pillows or bags easily on a sewing machine.

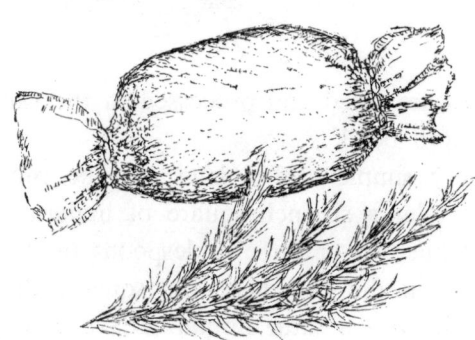

Balsam pillow.

Pomander Balls

Pomander balls have been popular for a long time. In *Love's Labor Lost,* Shakespeare mentions the "lemon stuck with cloves," which is one kind of pomander ball. In Shakespeare's time the pomander ball was carried in a little round perforated metal case. A sniff from time to time was believed to protect against pestilence. It probably obliterated the stench of the London streets for a moment or two as well. Sometimes a mixture of fragrant petals and herbs was carried in the little perforated ball or in a bag by the less well to do for the same purpose. Today pomander balls are most often Apples or citrus fruit covered with Cloves and placed in a net bag, tied with a ribbon, and used to perfume closets. The spicy odor lasts for years. Pomander balls are easy to make but a little tedious. Something for a rainy day.

To Make a Pomander Ball

You'll need

An Apple, Orange, Lemon, or Lime
¼ teaspoon Nutmeg
¼ teaspoon Cinnamon
¼ teaspoon powdered orrisroot
Several dozen whole Cloves
A plastic bag
An ice pick or other sharp instrument

Procedure

Put the Nutmeg and Cinnamon and orrisroot in the plastic bag.
Shake the bag to mix thoroughly, put aside.
Poke holes in the fruit with the ice pick following a circular pattern.
Push the Cloves into the holes. (This is the tedious part.)
When the fruit is completely covered, place in the plastic bag.
Shake vigorously.
Remove the fruit from the bag and shake or brush off excess powder.
Place the fruit in a cool dark dry place. A kitchen cupboard should be fine.
Leave for ten days to two weeks or longer.
The fruit feels hard and firm when dried completely.

The pomander ball can be used as is or covered with net as mentioned before. Just take a square of white net, place the

der balls.

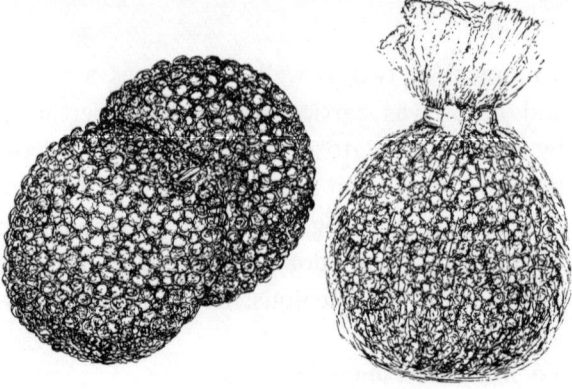

pomander ball in the center, bring up the corners, and tie with a satin bow. Make a long loop so the ball can be placed over a hanger.

Now, if you would like the fragrance of a spring morning in your home all year long, start with one or two fragrance projects and continue adding more fragrance from different sources from time to time.

Sachet of your choice can be placed in the linen closet and in dresser drawers and in the pillowcases on your beds. Tuck some under the mattresses. Place fragrance bags in the hems of your drapery and under sofa and chair pillows. Hang pomander balls made from different fruits in all your bedroom closets, Pine bags in the coat closet and in winter storage chests and drawers. Place uncovered pomander balls in fruit bowls and tuck them in kitchen drawers. Hang Sweet Woodruff or other herbs to dry in the kitchen, twining them around groups of hanging Gourds (see chapter on fruits and vegetables). Have bowls of dried herbs or potpourri jars all through the house, not forgetting the bath. Open them frequently. Most potpourri mixtures last for years and their fragrance can be revived with special preparations available from the drugstore or mail order. Make a bath sachet from one of the simple recipes given in this chapter, omitting the orrisroot and substituting borax in double the amount of orrisroot. Hang the sachet with a pretty ribbon from the hot water faucet for a refeshing bath. Add sprigs of dried and fresh herbs to flower and foliage bouquets. Finally cultivate fragrant plants and herbs in your window garden (suggestions can be found in the chapter on houseplants) and burn pine cones in your fireplace.

Mail Order Sources:

For pomander balls, potpourri mixtures in attractive jars, sachet, and all ingredients for fragrance projects:

Caswell-Massey Co., Ltd.
Catalogue Order Department
114 E. 25th St.
New York, N.Y. 10010

Chapter Ten

Decorating with Natural Materials

Fresh flowers and dried flowers, lush foliage, weathered wood, fruits and vegetables, pine cones, berries, and pods; all these treasures of the natural world can be used to add a very personal accent to your home. Like other accessories—paintings, art objects, small antiques, basketry, needlework, whatever appeals—they should harmonize with the total atmosphere. A pleasant bonus: You can be completely budget minded. If you collect or grow your own natural materials, you can achieve intriguing decorative effects at the lowest possible cost.

How do you start? Think of your home as the sum of its parts, with each part contributing some expression of your feeling toward life. Take stock of each area and room slowly. Look at the architectural features, the height of the ceiling, spacing of windows, the size of the area, and then look at the furnishings. What is needed? You may want to soften the bulk of a large chest. Is there a picture over the chest? Would a low wide container of foliage arranged with more height than width be just right to keep the picture in focus and balance the chest? You might prefer a footed bowl piled high with Gourds and glycerinized leaves to perform the same decorating function. In a tiny room, you may want to add color and interest with ceiling- and wall-hung containers of plants and flowers.

Think of containers and bases as the link between the natural materials and the style of your home, then choose those that are attractive and appropriate. Don't be limited by convention. The great variety of natural materials allows for an equal variety of containers and holders. Improvise containers from bird cages, lanterns, baskets of all kinds, teapots, soup tureens, pitchers, oil lamps, milk cans, crocks, silver gravy boats, tins and baking dishes, burls of wood, roots, antique boxes, candleholders, ash trays, and on and on. A list of mail order sources for attractive and unusual containers appears at the end of this chapter, but do visit antique shops and junk shops, hardware stores, decorating accessory shops, and craft outlets. Look at everything with an open mind. Become familiar with the innovative textures and shapes that ceramic craftsmen are producing in one of a kind jugs and pitchers and other articles that can be used for containers. Squat round candleholders with open sides through which the candlelight flickers will add charm to a patio dinner. At other times with a bouquet of flowers or a potted plant inside, they'll become handsome containers.

When you are arranging bouquets or groupings of natural materials, consider the compatibility of the plant material to its container and that of the container to the place where it will be displayed. To be decoratively effective, the arrangement must be in proportion to its surroundings, neither so large that it dominates or so small that it loses its decorative function entirely.

You can celebrate the changing of the seasons with natural materials even if you live where there is no change. This doesn't mean of course, that you limit yourself to dried arrangements in the fall and nothing but fresh flowers in spring. All the natural materials can be enjoyed the year round, but it's fun to change your decorating emphasis seasonally. Put away some of the dried and processed materials and rely more on fresh flowers and foliage when the world outside is generally doing the same. A table in an entry might be complemented by a large bouquet of fresh flowers in the summer. A large Boston Fern could replace it, if a planter of about the same size as the flower contained is used. In late fall a large bunch of red-berried Bittersweet with pressed autumn leaves could serve in the same spot. Evergreen branches could be enjoyed through the Christmas season, and when Christmas passed, January would be a good time in most areas to think about forcing branches. Cut the branches to size and enjoy the patterns their bare outlines create. When the branches burst into bloom: a lovely happening. While some of your natural accessories are changed with the season, others can remain as reminders of what has been and what is to come in the natural world. Dried Starflowers can add colorful accents to your home the year round. Dried Gourds are interesting accessories regardless of the season, and so are glycerinized leaves. A generous variety of natural materials will provide textural contrasts as well as contrasts of form and color that create visual pleasure and eliminate monotony.

You produce a feeling of order and completeness in your home with a judicious use of color. You will have instant harmony, for instance, if you place a bowl of orange Marigolds close to a few orange pillows, but more subtle complements can be achieved by picking up small bits of color in a room and matching them with an arrangement of flowers or fruit. The least noticeable color in a flowered print can be brought out by an arrangement of the same color placed across the room. Use color to brighten dim areas. Bright yellow has the greatest carrying power. To enliven a dark hall, you could fill a shining brass container that will catch and reflect any available light with a large bunch of yellow Chrysanthemums. A stoneware jug filled with Daisies, for instance, would not be nearly as effective a room brightener.

Consider color when you are entertaining. Flowers and fruit and other natural materials used in a table centerpiece should harmonize with the tablecloth or place mats, china, and other accessories. On an informal table, with perhaps yellow coarse-weave mats and orange napkins, the color scheme could be carried out quite adequately with yellow and orange flowers in a ceramic bowl. It might be more interesting to use Oranges and Lemons arranged in alternate tiers to form a pyramid arranged on a circle of flat green leaves, or you could group flowers and fruit casually around a curve of driftwood.

Natural materials can be used everywhere. At your front door, they will seem to extend your welcome outward and speak pleasantly of the family within. In some areas it is traditional in fall to tie several ears of dried corn together and hang them beside the door to commemorate the season. Fall decorations composed of colorful Gourds strung together with several branches of autumn leaves are timely and attractive too. Large floor-standing crocks and baskets can hold massive bouquets that are new with each season; for instance, dried grasses and Dock for fall, and Evergreens for winter; large branches of green foliage, with flowers when available, can be enjoyed at other seasons. Small Evergreens in planters can be placed on either side of architecturally formal doorways. Two wall planters, holding flourishing Ivy plants, can be placed together on one side of a formal entrance with pleasing results. Wrought-iron bird cage planters filled with glycerinized foliage or dried materials are delightful beside entries of many styles, a reminder of the Portuguese custom of hanging cages with live birds inside beside the front doors. Wall-hung baskets overflowing with flowers and vines are charming for cottages.

Patios and porches are natural habitats for Strawberry jars filled with herbs. Small trees in movable planters go here too, as well as hanging baskets with Petunias and Begonias cascading over the sides. Large pieces of artistically shaped driftwood will be right at home.

Entrance halls and foyers continue the impression formed outside your home. If space is limited, the area can be effectively decorated with ceiling- and wall-hung planters or with floor-standing containers of natural materials. If appropriate to the style of your home, plaques with designs of dried pods and cut pine cones or large dried flower "prints" can add interest to the walls. A touch of fragrance can be introduced here too. Several sprigs of Rosemary placed behind a picture or tucked into an arrangement will add subtly to the atmosphere.

Natural materials go in every room. Kitchens, no matter how compact or efficient, become cozy and charming when fragrant herbs and scented-leaved Geraniums are grown in a window planter. Gourds strung together with dried Woodruff and Strawflowers can add color and interest to the sides of cupboards.

An attractive permanent arrangement of dried flowers on the breakfast table can be rotated with a bowl of wild flowers or garden flowers when they are available.

Family rooms and informal areas can be decorated with large bouquets of dried Mullein and Goldenrod in floor-standing baskets. Driftwood displayed with polished stones is a handsome fireplace accessory. Feathers can be added to informal dried arrangements with interesting visual results.

Large bouquets of shining foliage can add warmth to the most formal room. Sparse oriental bouquets are appropriate to the same setting. Handsome jars of potpourri can lighten the atmosphere. On a coffee table a terrarium filled with blooming African Violets will add restrained color.

Bedrooms are charming with dried flower "prints" on the walls and tiny bouquets of fresh flowers arranged with fresh Mint on the night table. A miniature bouquet of dried flowers arranged under a dome can accent a writing table or small chest.

Dining rooms seem to call for fruits and vegetables either dried or fresh arranged in tiers or in footed bowls or on trays, depending upon the style of furnishings. A bowl of pomander balls on a sideboard will add a refreshingly spicy scent. For bright color, Geranium plants can be grouped beside the window.

Bathrooms used to be left pretty much to themselves. Now many of them seem to be blossoming out in Roman splendor. Enclosed gardens that for privacy can be entered only through the bath are becoming quite usual in new homes. Smaller bathrooms are charming with tiny Starflower bouquets color matched to other accessories. Even the smallest bath can be lush with ceiling-hung plants.

The photographs that follow show natural materials as an integral part of the decorating scheme. Most of the interiors have been designed by professional decorators. Hopefully they will provide ideas for you and your home.

May you have many pleasant hours experimenting, trying out new ideas, and enjoying the world of natural materials.

Walk into this delightful kitchen any morning and your spirits are bound to soar. Old-fashioned warmth is combined beautifully with the crisp efficient look of today. The window garden of herbs is the focal point of the room establishing a sense of the past with the choice and arrangement of the plants. The window treatment is imaginatively conceived. Adjustable shelves have been built in front of the two end windows. The shelves are easily removed and replaced so that the windows can be kept sparkling clean in the background. At night the plant forms are reflected in the clear glass. The plants have been placed, in their clay pots, inside matching white containers. Two hanging plants in similar but not matching ceramic containers grace the center window and carry the eye down to a planter where a flourishing Chives plant stands ready to be snipped. Single white containers hold additional herbs on either side. The entire garden is tied together by the scalloped cornice extending over all three windows. The walls of this attractive room have been decorated with care and reflect the owners' interests as well as their talent for assemblage. Notice how well the antique clock, a find at a country auction, relates to the long narrow cutting board beside it and to the mixing spoons of light-colored wood in their dark Walnut holder just below.

The objects on the open shelves above the multi-drawered cupboard have been arranged with equal care. Spices in a variety of containers from glass-stoppered bottles to small metal canisters to those found on the grocer's shelf have been grouped with those of like design in a precise manner that complements the pieces of fine antique china on the top shelf. A hodgepodge of spice jars would have seemed incongruous with the china.

Dark wood and dark wood tones have been used very effectively to introduce warmth into this predominately white kitchen. The warm accent made by the dark wood of the doors below the sink and by the dark wood of the cupboard is complemented by the handcrafted, coarse weave field basket, as well as the mortar and pestle on the counter top above. Antique arm chairs carry this on, and the choice of an old-fashioned print for the chair cushions is very much in the spirit of the room.

This cheerful kitchen is an excellent example of an integrated decorating scheme subtly executed to produce a desired effect.

In a small apartment, an open divider defines space functionally while creating a feeling of spaciousness. This handsome divider is composed of adjustable shelves in a variety of heights. The shelves can add decorative interest to either dining or living area or both. It is a definite plus for the dining area, which is simply the windowless end of a long narrow room. In a limited space, the divider provides a showcase for many of the things that interest the vibrant young couple who lives here. The arrangement of the shelves is carefully co-ordinated with the objects that are displayed and helps emphasize each interest, while at the same time contributing to the over-all decorative effect. The tall primitive sculpture of mother and child standing on the floor is balanced on one side by the lines of the branches just coming into bloom. These are held in place by a needlepoint holder anchored with clay to the floor of a low container. On the opposite side, the cloudlike mass of the dried plumes of Pampas Grass offers contrast to both sculpture and branches and provides balance with height. The bindings of books, whose titles suggest an interest in art and philosophy, add an accent of color. Some of the books have been covered with a screen-printed paper by the lady of the house to increase their decorative impact. The paper is cut to size and then glued over the uninteresting binding. Several coats of varnish are added for an antiqued effect. A very interesting hand-thrown ceramic container that could have held plant material, stands empty so that its form and design may be enjoyed without distraction. One senses the owner's interest in the form of objects by the way the objects have been displayed as well as in the choice of objects. The metal fish is a gracefully curved mass that subtly complements the grouping of glasses. The dining table all set and waiting is imaginatively centered with a container of Escarole leaves. The tips of the leaves have been cut off (and used in a forthcoming salad) leaving the bleached heart leaves of the vegetables to form this simple but attractive centerpiece.

A gently sloping cathedral ceiling and a long window bring light and architectural interest to this contemporary kitchen and dining area. The window wall highlights the woodland scene outside, dispelling any coldly functional effect. Simple matching shades co-ordinate the windows in both areas and emphasize the expanse of glass. Raising and lowering them to provide sun and glare control results in interesting geometrical patterns along this wall. The tall healthy fig tree, in a container that is completely appropriate to the surroundings, is placed well for its own health and for decorative effect against the wooded background. The casual bouquet of flowers on the kitchen counter lends a needed note of informality to the room. In the dining area, the round Saarinen table with matching swivel chairs provides contrast to the straight lines and angles of the counters and windows. It is attractively centered with a handcrafted wooden tray and bowl in which fruit—Apples, an Orange, a Lemon, and a Banana—are carefully placed with bunches of Grapes in an almost medieval design. Outside on the deck, potted flowering plants provide color for the interior while enjoying the effects of sunlight and fresh air. The hanging light fixtures in both areas are co-ordinated without matching and add to the crisp atmosphere of the room, which suggests that a marvelously efficient woman uses the functional desk in the corner. A love of order is as apparent in the arrangement of the fruit in the table centerpiece as it is in the design of the room. One imagines gourmet meals prepared with efficient precision in this environment.

Imagine slipping into a fragrant tub of water in this luxurious room? Adjoining is an enclosed and heated glass-ceilinged solarium that can be enjoyed visually through the glass windows and sliding glass door while one relaxes in the sunken tub. Here, houseplants hang at different levels and a Palm tree and Fern, as well as potted Tulips and Daffodils, grow and flourish. The unusual chaise invites you to linger awhile after your bath in the delightful, almost tropical, surroundings. In the bathroom itself an unusual stand of shelves holds towels and lotions and bath powder, as well as an antique potpourri jar and a small incense burner. The narrow shelves add a quaint and provocative accent to the exotic room. The idea could be borrowed for smaller bathrooms. For all their decorative interest the shelves do not occupy much space. On the floor of the bath near the glass window, Ferns are massed for a soft green contrast to the gleaming tiles. The plants will receive enough light for their needs from the solarium. On the counter next to the sink a charmingly casual bouquet of Daisies is a piquant accent in this sleek sophisticated atmosphere. A large abstract painting, reflected in the mirror, contrasts interestingly with the overtones of ancient Roman luxury. A smaller painting would be as appropriate in a smaller bathroom, and along with plant materials it could relieve the cold functional aspect inherent in most bathrooms.

An impression of oriental simplicity and naturalness is felt in this contemporary living room. The pale cypress wood used in the fretwork over the windows as well as in the construction of the tokonoma-inspired alcove contribute to this feeling. The natural shantung shades at the windows do too. The alcove itself is imaginatively conceived and its design creates a strong oriental impression. Notice the use of the bamboo support. The lower cupboards provide needed storage, but the upper section is used to further the oriental mood through the display of accessories. The owner has used a tall, casually arranged bouquet of Eucalyptus leaves to balance the Japanese print hung next to it. A tall Japanese flower arrangement would be appropriate here as well but not as long lasting as the foliage. The fragrant foliage bouquet relates well to the Japanese print and to the stacked lacquered food boxes, as well as to the other oriental articles placed on the shelf in a balanced arrangement. The built-in window wall continues the feeling of the orient in its clean lines of the campaign chests set snugly side by side and unified by a continuous surface of cypress wood. In one corner, a shelf holds one flourishing houseplant above another in an attractive container. The Philodendron climbing rapidly up a totem toward the first plant is a pleasing touch. The small cabinet on this counter complements the lacquered boxes in the tokonoma alcove as well as the general form of the campaign chests below. In front of the other window a very casually arranged vase of dried plant materials fills the space with its softly rounded form. Two woven wicker chairs with clean Scandinavian lines are in harmony with the atmosphere of this interesting room. All the plant materials contribute to its atmosphere of simplicity and naturalness.

This is a warm intimate room with a feeling of the past about it. The interior designer has mixed all kinds of styles, and instead of disaster has produced a very personal pleasant area. The natural brick wall and the oil-stained shuttered door complement each other beautifully. An off-center window is given importance through the use of a laminated shade in a bold floral design. The same floral is repeated in the upholstery of the French arm chair and the covering of one of the pillows on the velvet sofa. Above the shuttered door a false shade is co-ordinated with the shade on the window by the use of the same background color and appliqués of some of the floral heads. In this small room, this imaginative treatment is more interesting than a matching shade would be. Paintings in a variety of sizes and frames dispel any harshness that might be created by the brick wall. Especially eye-catching is the gilt-framed picture over the fireplace. Below it, the ornate brass container is an effective complement. The shining green of the long-lasting foliage is delightful against the soft red brick, and the arrangement can be moved off the hearth when a fire is wanted. In the window, the soft beige of the dried plant materials, picked on the stalk in the countryside, provides a foil for the vividness of the shade. A bouquet of Chrysanthemums, very casually arranged, adds a needed touch of color on the small table next to the sofa. Antique keys, a mysterious-looking box, and other personally interesting objects help the bouquet balance the large table lamp. The lamp incidentally harmonizes very well with the brass foliage container and the gilt picture frame. The entire rear wall appears wider than it is because of the visual effect of the shelves. Books chosen for their subject matter add incidental color and interest, along with the objects chosen for their appeal to the owners. The footed bowl of fruit high on a center shelf would be just as decorative on a lower shelf where the fruit could be enjoyed. Here, one is inclined to think that it may rot before anyone is inclined to climb up for a sample.

This charming patio, screened on three sides, is covered with translucent paneling that provides weather protection yet admits light. It is a delightful, easy-to-maintain, indoor-outdoor area. An impression of a secluded glen is created by the thoughtful arrangement of foliage and flowering plants. Hanging plants suspended at intervals from the ceiling are like living mobiles of green. A small square garden has been provided for plants and shrubs. Potted plants brought from the house can be enjoyed in this protected environment for extended periods. Enough light is available to make the garden plot practical, but watering must become a frequent routine. Meals in these surroundings are a pleasant experience that can be enjoyed frequently. Furnishings and table decorations can be left in place, protected from even a driving rain by easily lowered canvas shades. The table is set for a summer luncheon with a centerpiece of fruit arranged in a footed container. A Pineapple stands upright at one end of the container with Grapes and other fruits arranged casually beside it—not too imaginative but certainly appropriate. The limp leaves hanging over the rim of the container could have been kept crisp if the stem ends had been placed in a small piece of water-soaked Oasis, then wrapped in plastic and pushed out of sight inside the container. The candles in glass chimneys flanking the fruit arrangement are a handsome and practical touch. The glass protects the candles from any strong breezes and the size of the chimneys complements the rather imposing container. Glass chimneys incidentally can be used for various decorating effects. Another time, without candles they could be placed on rings of leaves and filled to the top with bright green Limes.

Here is a kitchen that has gone far beyond conventional concepts. The natural tree limb dominates the room and dictates its accessories and decorating style. The tree was, of course, put in place when the house was constructed, and the low breakfast bar was built around it at that time. Now the tree has become a hanger for cheese and salami and an interesting ceramic lantern as well as anything else the owners find amusing. Wood-tone paneling on existing wall surfaces and on the refrigerator carries on the outdoor theme of the room. On the shelf above the refrigerator a fine flourishing Ivy plant breaks the long line of the shelf and receives needed sun from the high windows. Ceramic serving pieces add a handcrafted accent in keeping with this room's theme. The owners, besides being friends of the natural world, are intrigued with the Orient. Without clashing with the dominant theme, they have introduced a small oriental corner next to the refrigerator—a charming idea that could be borrowed for more conventional kitchens. Here condiments are stored in the drawers of the tiny cupboard. In the niche between the small drawers, a sheaf of dried Wheat, with stems cut short and bound together, has been placed at an angle to fill the space. Its soft beige tone matches and blends with the wood of the interesting little cupboard. Across the room, on the pass-through shelf above the sink counter, an oversized bouquet is attractively but casually arranged in a handsome ceramic bowl, providing a needed splash of color. No detail has been overlooked in this fascinating room. Notice the three-legged stools of natural waxed wood; the oversized mugs, good for coffee or soup. Not surprisingly, a loaf of French bread and a square of cheese are the "centerpiece" for the late snack about to be enjoyed at the bar.

This dining room projects a rather formal impression, but informal accents have been introduced quite successfully. The window treatment is simple but pleasing. The print on the shades and lambrequin help to relieve some of the preciseness in the arrangement of the furniture. Two impressive paintings add a feeling of elegance to the room. For a lighter touch the chairs are deliberately unmatched. The two placed against the window are Queen Anne, but all four have rounded backs. The lowboy is a charming piece, and its curved legs further unify the room, repeating the curves of the chair backs and the round table as well as those in the shade print. A constant interchange of curves and rectangles (the lines of the window and picture frame, the top surface of the lowboy) is felt even if it isn't perceived and gives a feeling of balance to the room. The basket of fruit on the lowboy is an attractive accessory that could be enjoyed in many situations. It's very easy to do. The basket is an ordinary fruit basket that has been spray painted with several coats of paint and then varnished. Each application must be completely dry before the next is applied. Tightly crumpled tissue paper fills the basket, providing a rounded effect above the rim. This is covered with sheet moss and the fruit is placed on top. If you wish, wood picks can be pushed into one or two pieces of fruit to fasten them to the moss and tissue paper and permit them to hang over the side. The overflowing bouquet of flowers, centered on the dining table, is a perfect choice for this table and these surroundings. Crumpled chicken wire inside the container holds it in place. Such a large bouquet will need water added to the container every day.

This delightful corner of a small study seems to invite you to sit down awhile and enjoy its quiet charm. The grain of the Oak in the well-oiled antique secretary is as pleasant to observe as the quaint design of the piece. Next to it, a tall, odd-shaped barrel, a find from a day of antique hunting, holds dried materials from the roadside in casual disarray. All kinds of pods and Thistles and grasses are combined in a way that is reminiscent of their rangy growth beside a country road. Perhaps one or two of the long-stemmed pods should be pulled up a bit, but an arrangement that was too well staged would be out of place in this quiet corner. The wood-paneled wall provides just the right background. The clock above the dried plant "happening" balances the wall space between the tole lamp and the desk and contributes to the atmosphere of the area. The tole lamp and the reproduction of a deacons' bench continue the feeling, placed attractively in front of a window that is curtained and draped quite formally to preserve the closed away feeling of this quiet retreat.

A window shelf flanked by built-in shelves is an attractive solution to the space problem in this small kitchen. The entire unit provides needed storage as well as room for the decorative window garden of potted plants. This end of the room would have been dull and uninteresting without this treatment. On the window shelf, three Azalea plants in white pots add a splash of soft color. Beside them, on amusingly conceived plant stands, the dark green foliage of the two Ivy plants heightens the effect of the colorful flowering plants. The vertical blinds behind them provide a simple background co-ordinated to the functionalism of the small kitchen. Almost any other treatment, shutters, or curtains, would have seemed busy and would have visually diminished the already limited space. The serving cart is an ingenious solution for late-night snacks and pick-up lunches when the dining room doesn't seem worth the trouble. The shelves on either side of the window provide visual interest as well as storage space. One would wish that at least one or two had been used to simulate a shadow-box effect for a dried bouquet or a temporary fruit arrangement that could be nibbled while it provided a touch of natural color.

This rather small apartment living-dining room has an atmosphere of intimacy and charm created by the carefully planned decorating scheme. Without clutter, space has even been provided for the things the owners like to have around them. A visual feeling of spaciousness has been created by the window treatment which extends across the entire end wall. One large laminated paisley print shade and valance covers the three small windows. Two beams that form jogs on either side of the windows have been covered with felt to match the background of the shade print. In front of the windows a very interesting antique sewing table serves as a small writing table as well as a plant stand. Foliage plants are permanent accessories on the table with flowering plants added in season. The entire ensemble of two quaint Victorian chairs, the sewing table, and the wide window background provides a needed focal point for the room. To one side spears that are souvenirs of the owners' passion for travel stand in the corner. In front of them, a handsome handwoven basket, itself a travel remembrance, holds a large floppy bouquet of Wheat. The soft beige of the grain blends well with the room. Four separate sheaves of Wheat were individually bound and then placed together in the basket to fall into the casual arrangement that complements the background of spears. An interesting collection of candelabra displayed on one wall are balanced by a very strong abstract painting opposite. To one side, next to the upholstered chair, a foliage plant fills an end table with its vining leaves, balancing the effect of the plants by the window. The dining table is covered with a paisley print cloth that, with the paisley sofa cushions, unifies the decorating scheme. A tiny informal bouquet on the dining table adds a charming touch.

This gay country kitchen, opening to a patio, seems to have captured part of the out of doors in its wallpaper of screen-printed Ferns. Rough wood paneling and the dark wood trim add immeasurably to this woodland atmosphere. The charming Dutch door is in keeping with the rural feeling of the room. The counter top has been divided with wood beams into functional compartments, separating the flower arranging center near the back door from the culinary areas. Here, delightfully natural bouquets stand waiting to be placed in other areas of the home. The large window beside the door has been very simply decorated with a Roman shade laminated with the same fern print. The wicker magazine rack standing beneath the window is an innovative touch. It has been changed into an informal planter to hold the potted spring flowering bulbs about to burst into bloom. These will be replaced with foliage plants when their beauty has passed. The idea is delightful and readily adaptable to other rooms in other homes. A modern round globe lighting the dining table has been co-ordinated with the rustic atmosphere through the addition of the scalloped mesh shade. Beneath it, the round table is flanked with cane-backed chairs whose seat cushions repeat the Fern print. Centered on the table, a large overflowing bouquet in the casual style the lady of this house prefers adds needed warmth and color to the table and this side of the room. As most large bouquets are, it is held in place with crumpled chicken wire placed inside the container.

One corner of their family room has been turned into a library by these owners who are insatiable readers and collectors of books. The window behind the desk was a problem, but it has been handled beautifully. It faces a depressing scene which would have destroyed the mood of the room. The problem was ingeniously solved by covering the windows with Rice-paper panels. The room is air conditioned so that the windows need not be raised. Panels and shelves can be removed several times a year for cleaning. The shelves which line this end of the room continue around in front of the windows and have been attractively decorated with healthy plants and a few artifacts of interest to the owners. The light background silhouettes the leaves and the staggered placement of the plants highlights individual plants, increasing their visual impact. A crowded unimaginative placement of plants would not be nearly as effective and would have obstructed the light which is needed in this rather dark room. The top shelf has been left bare to admit more light, but it would have been more attractive with the addition of interesting small objects and at least one vining plant. The shelves around the wall have been handled well. The bindings of the books are colorful. No attempt has been made to co-ordinate them in a decorative sense. The owners are serious readers whose collection is pleasing, in itself, to them. Vases, bowls, small sculpture placed here and there among the books provides visual relief, breaking up the rows of books. The painting hung low inside the shelves is a good choice both in subject matter and in the frame. The ornate candleholder is a harmonious touch. On the desk the informally arranged bouquet of Roses is complementary to the painting and candleholder and serves a unifying function, relating the desk to the decorative walls.

The interests of the owners of this charming living room are apparent in their choice of accessories. Notice the small antique footstool beside the chair. On the wall, paintings, plaques, framed maps, and documents are arranged in an interesting pattern above the narrow chest. One can sense their affection for old and homey objects in their display of candleholders and odd bottles on the chest. Very much in keeping with the informality of the room is the naturally arranged bouquet of dried grasses and pods mixed with Goldenrod and other countryside collectibles. The arrangement placed in an old-fashioned wicker plant stand in one corner adds height to balance the high-ceilinged room and testifies to the owners' interest in natural materials and the out of doors. Most innovative is the camouflaged side window. Its unattractive view has been hidden behind three shelves. Here a graceful *Asparagus sprengeri* plant shares a shelf with an interesting assortment of odd bottles and antique jars. Below on the bottom shelf, which is actually the wide window sill, dried Starflowers are arranged beside another vigorous plant, whose bulk belongs on this lower shelf, balancing the airy grace of the *Asparagus sprengeri* above. Fresh flowers, distinctive vases, empty and filled, old plates, dried grasses, and a sprightly little plant placed in its own pot inside a marmalade crock complete the engaging display. The owners' interest in houseplants can be seen in their flourishing appearance, which can only be achieved through concerned care.

The distinctive choice of accessories and their thoughtful arrangement all contribute to the attractive individuality of this room. As they should, the natural materials add a final and appropriate touch.

Mail Order Sources:

Fran's Basket House
89 W. Main St.
Rockaway, N.J. 07866

Interesting baskets. Catalogue.

Downs
Evanston, Ill. 60204

Domes. Catalogue. Interesting articles to improvise for containers.

Floral Art
P. O. Box 394, Highland Sta.
Springfield, Mass. 01109

Vases and containers, including hollowed bamboo. Catalogue.

Garden Club Products
Mapes' Garden Center
Route 1, Kennebunk, Me. 04043

Many unusual containers. Catalogue.

Williamsburg Craft Center
Colonial Williamsburg, Inc.
Williamsburg, Va. 23185

Reproductions of colonial containers including delft finger vases. Catalogue.

Harriet Carter
Plymouth Meeting, Penna. 19462

Bird cage planters and other interesting containers. Catalogue.

The Ferry House
Dobbs Ferry, N.Y. 10552

Containers and interesting articles for improvisation. Catalogue.

A Personal Reading List

The Natural World:

Wandering Through Winter
Edwin Way Teale. Dodd Mead, New York, 1965.

North with the Spring
Edwin Way Teale. Dodd Mead, New York, 1951.

Journey into Summer
Edwin Way Teale. Dodd Mead, New York, 1960.

Autumn Across America
Edwin Way Teale. Dodd Mead, New York, 1956.

In Wildness Is the Preservation of the World
Selections from Thoreau. Photographs by Elliot Porter. Sierra Club—Ballantine Books, 1962.

Art:

The Flower Piece in European Painting
Introduction by Margarette Salenger. Harper, New York, 1949.

A Gallery of Flowers
Germaine Bazain, Thomas and Hudson, 1960.

Decorating:

An Illustrated History of Furnishing from the Renaissance to the Twentieth Century
Mario Pranz. George Braziller, New York, 1964.

Flower Arranging:

The Art of Arranging Flowers—A Complete Guide to Japanese Ikebana
S. Sato. Harry N. Abrams, Inc., New York, 1966.

New Horizons in Flower Arrangements
Myra J. Brooks. Photographs by Alice and John Roche. M. Barrows, Inc., New York, 1961.

Wildflowers in Your House
Josephine von Miklos. Doubleday & Company, Inc., New York, 1968.

Miniature Flower Arrangements and Plantings
Lois Wilson. D. Van Nostrand Co., New Jersey, 1963.

Herbs:

Herbs, Their Culture and Uses
Rosetta E. Clarkson. The Macmillan Co., New York, 1942.

Herbs to Grow Indoors
Adelma Simmons. Hawthorn, New York, 1969.

Herbs and the Fragrant Garden
Margaret Brownlow. Darton, Longman & Todd, London, 1963.

Herbal
Joseph Wood Krutch. G. P. Putnam's Sons, New York, 1965.

Houseplants:

The World Book of Houseplants
Elvin McDonald. The World Publishing Co., Ohio, 1963.

The Woman's Day Book of Houseplants
Jean Hersey. Simon & Schuster, New York, 1963.

Miscellaneous:

Handicrafts of the Southern Highlands
Allen Eaton. Russell Sage Foundation, 1948. Paperback edition published 1970, Dover Press.

The Gardener's World
Joseph Wood Krutch. G. P. Putnam's Sons, New York, 1959.

An Eighteenth-Century Garland
Louise B. Fisher. Colonial Williamsburg, Virginia, 1951.

The Flower World of Williamsburg
Joan Parry Dutton. Colonial Williamsburg and Holt, Rinehart & Winston, New York, 1962.

Flower Cookery, The Art of Cooking with Flowers
Mary MacNicol. Fleet Press Corp., New York, 1967.

Travels of William Bartram
Edited by Mark Van Doren. Paperback edition, Dover Publications, 1955.

The History, the Beauty, the Riches of the Gardener's World
Josephine von Miklos and Evelyn Fiore. Random House, Inc., New York, 1969.

Index of Illustrations

Airlie Gardens, Wilmington, North Carolina (Department of Conservation and Development, North Carolina).	*12*
Tyron Palace, New Bern, North Carolina (Department of Conservation and Development, North Carolina).	*15*
Plan for a cutting garden.	*17*
Wheat.	*19*
Wild Ginger.	*19*
Gourd and Corn.	*19*
Wooded land in the fall (Vermont Development Department).	*21*
Stone Soldier Pottery, Jacksonville, Vermont (Vermont Development Department).	*23*
The Loom Room, Durham, North Carolina (Department of Conservation and Development, North Carolina).	*24*
Rose lively (The Wayside Gardens Company).	*30*
Heartsease.	*32*
Tuzzie-muzzie.	*34*
Casual arrangement (Witch Hill) (Ken Marsh).	*36*
Colonial arrangement for Williamsburg (Colonial Williamsburg photograph).	*38*
Mid-century hybrid Lilies (Oregon Bulb Farm).	*41*
Calendula (George Park Seed Company).	*43*
Mass bouquet from the ballroom of the Governor's Palace in Williamsburg (Colonial Williamsburg photograph).	*44*
Gladioli.	*45*
Earthenware vases.	*46*
Tall natural bouquet.	*47*

Tall Japanese bouquet.	*47*
An effective arrangement of a single Iris.	*47*
Brightening up a breakfast room (Window Shade Manufacturers Association).	*48*
The light touch in a study corner (Thomasville Furniture).	*50*
Dried flower arrangement (Customwood Manufacturing Company).	*52*
Chinese Lanterns.	*54*
Hanging basket of Strawflowers and Ivy.	*55*
Drying room (Colonial Williamsburg photograph).	*58*
Flower print with Pansies.	*68*
Flower print of dried flowers and pods.	*68*
Colonial bouquet (Colonial Williamsburg photograph).	*70*
Wiring Strawflowers.	*71*
Colonial arrangement of dried flowers.	*73*
Domed bouquet.	*75*
Wild flowers in a standing bouquet (Customwood Manufacturing Company).	*76*
Dried Mullein in a floor-standing arrangement (Syroco).	*77*
Grove of trees (Ken Marsh).	*80*
Sparse oriental arrangement.	*82*
Foliage arrangement.	*83*
Grasses (George Park Seed Company).	*84*
Arrangement of flowering branches.	*86*
Bare branches fill an empty corner (Window Shade Manufacturers Association).	*88*
Pussy Willows add charm to an informal room (Ethan Allen).	*89*
Wall-hanging arrangement of foliage.	*90*
Drying Pussy Willows.	*94*
Arranging dried grasses.	*94*
Silver bowl with foliage and Christmas ornaments (Reed & Barton).	*96*
Aucuba foliage arrangement (Henredon).	*97*
A basket of mixed foliage.	*98*
Ivy in an apothecary jar (Ken Marsh).	*102*

Gardening on the terrace (Potted Plant Information Center).	*106*
Aspidistra plant (U. S. Department of Agriculture).	*106*
Leafy plants for the house (U. S. Department of Agriculture).	*108*
Boston Fern.	*111*
A centerpiece of Geraniums.	*112*
Parsley in a stoneware crock.	*114*
Cacti (George Park Seed Company).	*118*
A small dish of Cacti.	*118*
Violets in a terrarium.	*119*
Hanging plants.	*121*
Wire plant stand holding flowering plants adds a garden effect (Window Shade Manufacturers Association).	*122*
Built-in planter (Potted Plant Information Center).	*123*
Gourds, Pumpkins, and driftwood (Vermont Development Department).	*126*
Basket of possibilities (George Park Seed Company).	*128*
An arrangement of fruit.	*129*
An eighteenth-century arrangement of fruit (Colonial Williamsburg photograph).	*131*
A colorful accent to the dining area (U. S. Plywood, Champion Papers).	*132*
Oriental arrangement of fruit.	*133*
Apples and Ivy.	*135*
Autumn centerpiece (Reed and Barton).	*135*
Asparagus and flowers.	*137*
Broccoli in a basket.	*137*
Wreaths of Peppers.	*139*
A cornucopia.	*140*
Driftwood (Bob Baugh).	*144*
The Presnells at work (Department of Conservation and Development, North Carolina).	*146*
Carved molding (Ken Marsh).	*147*
Thorned branches and fruit arranged orientally.	*148*

Sea-washed driftwood (Ken Marsh).	*150*
Pruning driftwood.	*152*
Bamboo trunk and flowers.	*154*
Driftwood and rocks.	*154*
Driftwood arranged with flowers and leaves.	*155*
Switchy branches in a standing arrangement.	*156*
Root with flowers.	*157*
Holiday decorations (Southern Highland Handicraft Guild).	*160*
Storing pottery (Department of Conservation and Development, North Carolina).	*162*
Handcrafted toy (Department of Conservation and Development, North Carolina).	*163*
Pine cone flowers.	*166*
Wiring a pine cone.	*166*
A basket of pine cones and sprigs of leaves.	*167*
Pine cones and flowers.	*168*
Long-stemmed pine cone flowers.	*169*
Making a pine cone wreath.	*171*
Boxwood and fruit in a pine cone wreath (Colonial Williamsburg photograph).	*172*
A print of pine cone flowers.	*175*
French potpourri jar (The Metropolitan Museum of Art. Gift of R. Thornton Wilson in memory of Florence Ellsworth Wilson, 1950).	*176*
Medieval still room (New York Botanical Garden Library).	*179*
Herbs.	*180*
Herb bowl (George Park Seed Company).	*181*
Silver pomander (The Metropolitan Museum of Art. Gift of Arthur Curtiss James, 1920).	*184*
Rose.	*186*
Rosemary.	*187*
Balsam pillow.	*188*
Pomander balls.	*190*
Christmas decorations in Williamsburg (Colonial Williamsburg photograph).	*192*

Early American kitchen with hanging plants in the window (Armstrong Cork Company).	*198*
Living room divider in a modern decor (Dorfile Manufacturing Company).	*200*
Breakfast room (Window Shade Manufacturers Association).	*202*
Bathroom and solarium (Tile Council of America).	*204*
Conversation area with an oriental touch (Window Shade Manufacturers Association).	*206*
Cozy living room with a mixed decor (Window Shade Manufacturers Association).	*208*
Screened terrace with small garden (Celanese Corporation).	*210*
Spacious kitchen with the feeling of the out of doors (Armstrong Cork Company).	*212*
Dining area (Window Shade Manufacturers Association).	*214*
Rustic corner for reading or writing (Syroco).	*216*
Small kitchen (Window Shade Manufacturers Association).	*218*
Bright living-dining room (Window Shade Manufacturers Association).	*220*
Bringing the garden into the kitchen (U. S. Plywood, Champion Papers).	*222*
Brightening up a den (Royal System).	*224*
A garden corner for the living room (Window Shade Manufacturers Association).	*226*

Index of Color Plates

Adding color to a dining area (Window Shade Manufacturers Association).
Brightening up a dark room (Camino Real by Thomasville).
Dried flowers over fireplace (Syroco).
Complementing the wood surfaces with plants (Customwood Manufacturing Company).
Natural materials used to bring out the colors (Flintcote).
Breakfast room and garden (Window Shade Manufacturers Association).
Flowers and fruit used to complement the deeper colors of furniture (Window Shade Manufacturers Association).
Dogwood branches emphasizing spaciousness (Charisma by Thomasville).
Foliage helps to emphasize the color scheme in study (Window Shade Manufacturers Association).
Baskets of flowers bring color to quiet areas (Flintcote).

Index of Nature Craft Projects
(Mail Order Sources Appear After Each Chapter)

	Page
Materials:	13
Sampling of Plants to Cultivate for Decorating	14
Seasonal Calendar for Collecting and Processing Natural Materials	26
Fresh Flowers:	31
The Language of Flowers (Tuzzie-muzzie)	35
Conditioning Cut Flowers	38
Arrangement	44
Dried Flowers:	53
Air Drying	59
Drying Flowers in an Agent	62
Pressing Flowers	65
How to Make a Flower Print	67
Arrangement	70
Gifts	75
Foliage:	81
Conditioning	85
Forcing	87
Preserving by Glycerinization	90
Press Drying Foliage	92
Cut Life and Preserving Techniques	98
Houseplants:	103
General Houseplant Culture	104
Simple Plant Propagating	105
Growing Foliage Plants	108
Flowering Plants	112
Plants for the Kitchen	114
Miniatures	117

	Page
Terrariums	*119*
Hanging Baskets	*120*
List of Decorative Plants	*124*

Fruits and Vegetables: *127*
    Arrangement — *127*
    Selecting and Conditioning — *134*
    Drying — *137*
    Decorative Ideas for Dried Vegetables — *141*
    Miniatures — *141*

Driftwood: *145*
    Treating and Conditioning — *151*
    Decorative Ideas — *153*
    Miniatures — *158*

Pine Cones: *161*
    Drying and Conditioning — *165*
    Cutting Pine Cone Flowers — *165*
    Accessories Made from Pine Cones — *167*
    Wreaths — *170*
    Plaques — *173*
    Miniatures — *174*

Fragrance: *177*
    Herb Bowl — *178*
    Potpourri — *181*
    Sachet — *186*
    Balsam Pillows — *188*
    Pomander Balls — *188*